Quotes from Car

"We will keep praying our hearts out for all of you. Thank you so much again for all of the information, the updates, the laughs, and the tears both of sadness and of joy. You have touched the lives of so many and you all are an inspiration to everyone!"
   —*Kirsten, Wisconsin*

"All of you are amazing! I have grown personally from your journaling and experiences…Thank you. I firmly believe that we must do our very best and trust our 'higher power' for the rest…your journey has reflected this strongly."
   —*Steph, Wisconsin*

"…between the laughter and the tears, I'm exhausted! Ken, it is amazing to read what you write. It makes me feel like I'm right there."
   —*Debbie, Illinois*

"I find inspiration in your 'story' because it is filled with love, devotion, understanding, courage, patience, friendship, resolve, and faith. May you find peace in healing."
   —*Kari, Minnesota*

"You certainly know how to get your message through with some very powerful words… I need to dry my eyes and return to work."
   —*Maggie, Wisconsin*

"Congratulations! Life is so special, and your journey has been an inspiration to all of us."
　　—Don and Deon, Wisconsin

"I'm typing this with tears running down my cheeks after reading all the wonderful messages from others. It is amazing how much love is surrounding you both."
　　—Alice, Wisconsin

"Good luck with your recovery. My husband is currently awaiting a liver transplant too. Your story has given me much needed hope at a time when things have been looking down. Thanks for sharing your story."
　　—Donna, Wisconsin

"I am utterly amazed at what you have done and hope and pray for you all. The amount of courage, trust, and love is unfathomable."
　　—Justine, Wisconsin

"Your approach to life and living each day to the fullest is truly an inspiration."
　　—Gary, Wisconsin

"You are both very special people who have touched and helped shape so many lives."
　　—Amy, Minnesota

Transplanted

A Love Story

Kenneth C. Becker, DEd

K. Becker

2007

Transplanted: A Love Story

Published by Wheatmark™
610 East Delano Street, Suite 104, Tucson, Arizona 85705 U.S.A.
(888) 934-0888 ext. 3
www.wheatmark.com

ISBN: 978-1-58736-897-4
LCCN: 2007930376

For Peg, a very courageous woman
who never allowed herself to be a victim,

For Gretchen and all organ donors who are loving enough,
and courageous enough to give of themselves
in a most profound way,

and

For Jade, Logan, Ava, and Molly—our future.

ACKNOWLEDGMENTS

To acknowledge all who have helped us on this journey is an impossible task. However, to not make the attempt would be equally impossible. And so I do so only with the fear that I have not mentioned all those who have assisted us.

Gretchen Beckstrom is our hero. How can one possibly thank someone for saving your life or the life of the person you love? There are no words. Know that your love, generosity, and courage are beyond compare. You have given Peg life.

The staff at Mayo Clinic in Rochester, Minnesota, made Gretchen's gift a reality. From the surgeons to the secretaries, all have made this painful experience as painless as possible. We thank you all. I must give a special and heartfelt thanks to our Dr. John Poterucha. When all was lost, you gave us hope. Your gentle hand continues to guide us on our way. And hallelujah to Chaplain Mary Johnson. We met you immediately after Peg's first diagnosis, and you have been with us ever since. Your guidance and your humor have been our saving grace.

To our families who have made this effort worthwhile. We are here because you were there. And to Peg's sister and my "go-to" person, Jane Robertson—you have been with us for every step of this journey. How very comforting to have you at our side and covering our back. Thanks for hanging in there with us.

To all our friends for which another book could be written: our friends in Wisconsin and Arizona and across the country, our former students, and friends of friends. You expressed your love and caring in so many ways that we are humbled and overwhelmed. Thank you all for your support and kind words when they were needed the most. And thanks so very much to Geri and John Coggins for providing us with our home away from home and to Barb Rasmus for your twin cities respite both physically and emotionally. Also, to Roger and Julie Deets for your friendship and support. You helped to relieve some fears when there were almost too many to bear. Thanks so very much to Kari Etrheim for the good food, for your wonderful friendship, and for the most appreciated trip to the emergency room one dark and snowy night. And a five-star telephone salute to Mary Lawrence, Mary Esten, and Geri Coggins for all the phone calls and long, long, long conversations with Peg. I still wonder what it is that you spend so much time talking about. And to Pat Keyser, a 7 No-Trump Contract is awarded for your support and encouragement in writing this book and in helping us to improve our bridge game, at times both of which seemed like an insurmountable undertaking. A special thanks to Serene Rein, Barb Rasmus, and Jane Robertson for reviewing and editing the manuscript. Your assistance in this project was invaluable. How lucky can a person be to have such friends?

Professional photographer Jill Chumas took pictures of the gals at "camp," and Jane Robertson helped us keep a visual record of our experience at the hospital and the Gift of Life Transplant House. Many thanks.

A great big hug of appreciation for all the generous people who contributed to the National Transplant Assistance Fund on behalf of Peg and Gretchen. Your donations were a great help to us.

And finally, I'd like to thank Grael Norton, Lori Sellstrom, and the folks at Wheatmark Publishing for their optimistic and encouraging advice from start to finish that has turned my dream into that which you now hold in your hands.

My apologies for not mentioning everyone by name. To attempt to do so would be to court disaster by leaving someone out, and I cannot do that!

With so much love expressed by so many, Peg and I are blessed.

FOREWORD

I first met Peg and Ken when I had moved temporarily to La Crosse, Wisconsin, to be with and support my beloved mother as she took her own journey through cancer. Peg and Ken were her neighbors at the time, and my mother and I were the beneficiaries of their kindness, generosity, and compassion. Peg's diagnosis came less than two years after my mother's death. I recall being struck by the realization that Peg had undiagnosed cancer when she was giving so freely of herself to us. None of us knows if or when we might be called upon to endure such a journey.

Transplanted: A Love Story opens a window to the difficult and soulful journey that can unfold when cancer therapies fail, leaving organ transplantation as the final hope. The challenges are relentless on all levels of life—physical, emotional, psychological, and spiritual. This is a complex story, told through simple, heartfelt language. Ken's retrospective observations, woven together with chronological entries from their Caring-Bridge journal, tell a truly inspirational story about the sustaining power of love. The story is personal, but its messages are universal.

For those who may be asked to travel a similar journey, this book offers some tips—tips for dealing with the loss of control, for living while in the grasp of waiting for the next medical report, for understanding and sharing one's feelings, and for trying to make sense of intricate information when one's mind is frozen in grief and fear. If you can imagine yourself as a live organ donor, you will gain a glimpse into the mystery and magnitude of the gift you might someday give to another.

Ken's raw, uncensored accounting of their journey is also a story about survival. It teaches us how to do more than cope; indeed, it teaches us how to keep living while in the midst of life-shattering turmoil and uncertainty. It teaches us why we should not give advice to others who may be going through their own such journey. It teaches us about the power (and necessity) of hope. It teaches us (big time) about the value of humor in situations that are anything but funny. You will weep quietly, and you will laugh out loud. This book will touch you in many ways.

Throughout their ordeal, Peg has faced the demons of her cancer with a courage and grace that can come only from within. My deepest hope is that Peg and Ken's journey has turned the corner to a new path—a path that gives them the gift of time, time to share a gentle peace. Clearly, they already know how to live and love.

A friend and admirer,
Barbara Rasmus
September 2006

TABLE OF CONTENTS

"The Journey"

where are you going I asked
to places I have never been
was the answer
what do you plan to do I asked
my purpose will be evident at journey's end
who has planned your itinerary I asked
its plan will be revealed at times most unlikely
why would you consent to such a vague plan I said
I accepted the challenge
when I accepted life was the answer

—Mary Eleanore Rice
Images—Women in Transition, compiled by Janice Grana

INTRODUCTION

My wife, Peg, is a liver transplant survivor, and so am I. She had the surgery. I am her caregiver. This book is written in the hope that the journey we have taken may be helpful to others with a life-threatening illness. I believe the messages contained herein apply not only to transplant recipients, but also to others who may be facing a serious health crisis. The challenge is not simply surviving, but surviving with hope and with humor and with a life filled with meaning.

When Peg was initially diagnosed, we were living in La Crosse, Wisconsin. We were both retired professors teaching at the University of Wisconsin-La Crosse. After retirement, we became "snowbirds" and escaped the Wisconsin winters by retreating to sunny Arizona. Although we might have chosen to be treated elsewhere, we both felt confident and comfortable with the services offered at Mayo Clinic in Rochester, Minnesota. We continued treatment at Mayo Rochester from first diagnosis to eventual liver transplant and aftercare.

I have written this book with a two-pronged approach. All entries with a date attached are from the CaringBridge website. CaringBridge is a free, online service that connects patients with family and friends. It is a wonderful way to communicate with others without spending hours on the phone, repeating the same message over and over again. It also offers friends and relatives the chance to respond in the Guest Book section. Some of these responses are included throughout the book. My comments in CaringBridge were usually written late at night and at the end of exhausting days. The other entries you will read are my thoughts and reflections in retrospect. These are my attempts at making sense out of this very scary and very wonderful part of our lives.

Additionally, I need to comment on my use of "I" and "we." From first prognosis to the transplant and beyond, Peg and I have always felt that we have been taking this journey with each other. Therefore, I use the term "we" purposefully and intentionally, and the term "I" when appropriate. Being fully aware of the potential misuse of the term "we" as a way to speak for another, I can only say that "we"—Peg and I—have been, are, and forever will be in this together. "We" seems most appropriate most of the time.

A timeline of the events as they unfolded are included in Appendix A.

And so I begin.

Ken

Believe It or Not

The conclusion is always the same:
love is the most powerful and still the most
unknown energy in the world.

—Pierre Teilhard De Chardin
stronger than cancer, by Connie Payton

"*It might be* cancer." Hearing these words changed our lives forever and started us on a journey that we never could have imagined. The date was September 18, 2001, one week after 9/11. Not a good time. My wife, Peg, was in the Gundersen Lutheran Hospital Emergency Room in La Crosse, Wisconsin, with constant, severe pains in her abdominal area.

The preliminary diagnosis was diverticulitis, which is an inflamation of the walls of the colon. Almost as an afterthought, the emergency room physician decided to do a CT scan. That's when we got the news.

We immediately thought there had been a mistake. This couldn't be happening to Peg. Peg has always made healthy lifestyle choices, not only because she believed in living that way, but primarily because cancer was very prevalent in her family history. And so our journey of discovery began.

Peg's cancer was diagnosed as carcinoid that had spread or metastasized to her liver. The staff of our local medical center said that they had limited experience with this type of cancer. We asked to be referred to the Mayo Clinic in Rochester, Minnesota.

Thirteen days after those four little words "it might be cancer" were spoken, Peg had exploratory surgery in a search for the origin of the cancer cells or the primary site.

A liver transplant was the furthest thing from our minds when this all began. At every step of the way, we optimistically expected a cure. Surely some treatment would be available. Not a single one was, and three-and-a-half years later we found ourselves in the Transplant Center at Mayo Clinic.

This is the story of that journey. It is a story that I recorded daily on the website CaringBridge. It is our story. It is a love story. It is a true story. It only feels like a dream.

Didn't Work ... Again

"Hope is like water.
None of us can survive long without it."

—*Sweet Reprieve*, by Frank Maier

ow many times on this journey have we received bad news? More than I care to remember. With the original diagnosis, we were devastated. Cancer? Metastasized cancer? Cancer of the liver? How scary. With each treatment, we hoped for the best and received only the worst. Nothing worked. Every time a treatment failed, we had to try a different one.

The first attempt at treatment was "watchful waiting"—wait and see what happens. The tumors grew in size and number. Didn't work.

Then there were hormonal treatments. More tumors and larger tumors. Didn't work.

We tried chemotherapy. Same story—larger and more tumors. Didn't work.

Next was a clinical trial with an experimental drug called Iressa. Again, the tumors continued to grow and multiply. Didn't work.

With each and every failure, our reaction was shock and disappointment. We felt helpless, and the black cloud that hung over us grew bigger and darker. We were learning to live as best we could with heavy feelings that we couldn't escape. Death and loss and grief were our constant companions during these excruciatingly long, slow days. How does one continue to function when these dreadful thoughts of dying are always present? How does one survive when survival seems so impossible?

These were difficult days not only because of the emotional toll but also because of the physical toll. After each treatment, Peg lost energy. Some days, brushing her teeth required too much energy to complete in one act. Just getting out of bed was a struggle. With each treatment failure came the physical consequences of cancerous tumors devouring her liver. With each treatment failure came the increasing drain on her energy and on her fitness level.

Peg was wasting away not only from the cancer but also from the inactivity brought on by her lack of energy. She spent many days in bed with what were called "tumor fevers." These fevers were not caused by infection but rather by her body's reaction to the foreign invaders called carcinoids.

Peg struggled to live with the physical consequences of this disease, and we both struggled to live with the emotional consequences. The feeling of devastation was always there. The only way out was through hope.

Thank You, Officer No. 11

Hurdles are in your life for jumping.

—Rev. Sharon Pointdexter
stronger than cancer, by Connie Payton

Back in my college days, I ran the hurdles on our track-and-field team—the 120-yard high hurdles and the 220-yard low hurdles. Today, these races are run in meters with different distances and finishing times. However, the challenge remains the same—clear all the hurdles without falling and get to the finish line.

Going through the transplant-approval process is like running a hurdles race. At the start of the race, as you crouch down in the starting blocks, you cannot actually see the finish line, but you know it is there. Your heart begins to beat faster as you anticipate the gun. All you can see is the first hurdle, then you hear "On your mark, get set" —*bang!* Go! Run to the first hurdle and clear it, only to have another hurdle to clear. Hurdle after hurdle, you race down the track. You know the finish line lies ahead, but you have to take care of the immediate business at hand—clear the next damn hurdle. Hopefully, you clear them all and reach the finish line. Hooray!

That is exactly what hoping and waiting for a liver trans-

plant is like. You need a new liver: On your mark, get set—
bang! Go! Only in this race, you don't know exactly what all
the hurdles are and how many there may be, but you know
that the finish line—a successful liver transplant—is out there,
waiting.

All you can do is clear the hurdle in front of you and hope
you don't fall. Clear hurdle number one. What's next? Hurdle
number two. Clear hurdle number two. Get ready for hurdle
number three, and so it goes.

Early in this liver hurdle race, we had cleared our first
hurdle. Peg was given the go-ahead to proceed with the trans-
plant-evaluation process.

It was a clear sunny afternoon, and we were driving back
to Eau Claire, Wisconsin, from Mayo in Rochester, Minnesota.
We were excited. I was excited, and I was driving fast. The road
to Eau Claire is a two-lane, hilly affair, and as I sped over the
top of a hill on my way to the valley below, a police car, moving in my direction, appeared at the crest of the next hill. As I
watched, the red and blue lights suddenly came on. I knew he
had me, and I didn't care. Nothing was going to spoil today
and our good news. Ticket be dammed, I was happy.

I pulled off to the side of the road, opened the window, and
got my license out of my wallet, awaiting the inevitable as the
squad car turned around and parked behind me with lights
flashing. It went something like this:

Officer No. 11: Where are you going?

Me: Eau Claire, officer.

Officer No. 11: Is this your car?

Me: No, sir, it's a rental.

Officer No. 11: Where do you live?

Me: Arizona.

Officer No. 11: Do you know how fast you were going?

Me: No, Officer, but I guess I'm a little excited. We just left Mayo Clinic with the news that my wife was approved for a liver transplant.

Officer No. 11: Can I see your license, please?

I handed him my license, and he walked to the back of the car as we waited. He had me cold. I must have been doing at least seventy miles per hour in a fifty-five zone. I didn't care. Nothing was going to spoil this day. Peg had been approved to go forward in the process for the liver transplant. I was happy!

Officer No. 11 returned to the car window with paper in hand. Surprise. It wasn't a speeding ticket; it was a warning. All he said was "Good luck," then turned around and left us. "Good luck" was all he said. This was a good omen. This was the start of something wonderful. This was icing on the cake. Good luck!

I saved the warning ticket, and it is permanently displayed on the first page of the journal we kept to record our journey.

Thank you, Officer No. 11.

CaringBridge Website
Monday, December 6, 2004

This morning, I was serving as assisting minister at St. Paul's Lutheran Church in La Crosse. As the pastor and I were about to enter the church, a dear friend of many years came up to me and asked, "Al, would you add another petition to the prayers this morning? Our daughter is going to have surgery on Wednesday—she is donating two-thirds of her liver to…"

"Roger!" I said. "She's donating it to our good friend Peg!" I had never connected Roger and Lori with Gretchen. …Knowing that Gretchen is the daughter of Roger and Lori answers all sorts of questions about why Gretchen has chosen to do this. She comes from a most giving family!

CaringBridge Guest Book
Al and Julie, Arizona

After a three-year-and-four-month journey, we have come to December 22, 2004. This is the date of our surgery at Mayo Clinic in Rochester, Minnesota, when Peg will receive the gift of Gretchen's liver. Peg can expect to be in the hospital from ten days to two weeks. After that, she must be in the Rochester, Minnesota, area for four to six weeks as she recovers.

Gretchen can expect to be in the hospital for up to a week and then in Rochester for another week. Both Peg and Gretchen will be staying at the Gift of Life Transplant House once they are released from the hospital. Both Peg and Gretchen, as you can imagine, are excited and scared.

This is quite a life-changing experience they are about to begin. The entire surgical procedure is expected to last about ten hours—three to four hours for Gretchen and about six hours for Peg.

Ken

CaringBridge Website
Friday, December 10, 2004

We have a date for the surgery: December 22. If a deceased donor organ suddenly becomes available for another patient, however, there is a chance that Gretchen and Peg's surgery would have to be rescheduled. Deceased donor liver recipients have a window of opportunity of six hours for transplantation, so expediency of the surgery is of paramount importance. If such a situation arises, Peg and Gretchen would have to be rescheduled. We certainly hope that does not happen because there has been much planning for that date. We are told that a cancellation of a scheduled surgery occurs about 20 percent of the time. Keep your fingers crossed and say a prayer. If we are cancelled, we can certainly appreciate the urgency of the situation for someone else.

Did you know that the liver in both Peg and Gretchen will grow to about 90 percent of its full size within two to three weeks? Amazing! Within a year, both organs will grow to about 95 percent of their original size. They never will reach 100 percent. Amazing! The liver and the skin are the only two organs of the body to regenerate themselves. Amazing!

In Greek mythology, the gods punished Prometheus for giving men the gift of fire by sending an eagle to peck out his liver each night. During the day, it would grow back, only to be pecked out again the next night. Seems the ancient Greeks might have known more about human physiology than we thought. Amazing!

I will keep you posted.

Ken

Hoping and Wishing and Waiting

Please, God, give me patience, but do it now.

"A Wee Thought" by Mary Cathrine Smyth

The name of the game in this transplant business is hoping, wishing, and waiting. These we did a lot. It seems that waiting and hoping is what you do most of the time, except when you are terrified. We had quite a selection of emotional options, but no one said this was going to be easy. From day one, it seemed that we were waiting—waiting for test results, waiting for a doctor's approval, waiting for the latest blood draw results so we could proceed. Waiting, waiting, waiting.

Our entrée into this waiting game began with Peg's first liver biopsy. From that point on, we waited to see if the latest treatment of choice was working. After four unsuccessful treatments and a lot of waiting, we faced the last and perhaps the most difficult of all waiting periods. Because all of our options were spent, the only one that remained was a transplant. This was our one and only hope. If this option didn't succeed, there were none left.

The preliminary screenings were completed, and Peg and I were in our rental car on the way to the airport as we waited for the results. The cell phone rang. I answered and hoped for the best. Our doctor, Dr. Poterucha, asked to speak to Peg. I just knew from the sound of his voice that it was good news, and I was right. They had performed a PET scan to determine if there was cancer anywhere else in Peg's body. If there was, the process would have stopped. No further cancer was detected, and she was cleared to proceed.

I will always remember driving silently, waiting for the news, hoping for good news, wishing for the best. I will always remember driving silently with tears of joy and relief. This was the first of many life-or-death decisions upon which we had to hope and wish and wait.

Peg had to undergo more extensive testing before she would receive a go-ahead. The next step was to find an appropriate liver. Our doctors informed us early on that a deceased liver was not an option for Peg because of her particular diagnosis. Carcinoid cancer patients usually do not rate high on the MELD scale. The MELD scale is a screening test used to place prospective transplant recipients on a list that is prioritized according to need and potential for success. The higher the MELD score, the better the chance of receiving a liver. Not everyone who needs a liver receives one.

According to the Mayo Clinic, approximately 17,500 people were waiting for liver transplants in 2004. Sadly, most of these people have not received a life-saving organ. Of those on the waiting list, perhaps five thousand people actually received livers.

Our only hope was a live donor. As has been the case for us from the beginning, this too was not easy or quick. Mayo Clinic, Rochester, follows a very strict protocol for live donors. One requirement is that no one over the age of fifty-five is eligible. That eliminated both myself and Jane, Peg's sister. After many attempts to plead our case we finally got the message: *No is no!* No exceptions. I am happy, and at the same time sad, to report that the clinic rejected about fifteen other offers for various reasons, mostly due to age and mostly from our peer group. The transplant program at Mayo, Rochester, is very conservative and very cautious about putting a healthy person's life at risk.

So we hoped and wished for an appropriate younger donor. But we could not ask anyone to do this. How could we? Being a live donor is not an easy thing to do. It could be life threatening. The latest national statistic as quoted by Mayo is that one out of one hundred live donors does not survive the operation. Mayo has not lost a live donor yet, but the possibility still exists. All we could do was to put the word out and hope for the best.

We were very fortunate in that we had two live donors approved for the early stages of the screening process. One, my son Karl, was eliminated on the second day of testing because of medical reasons. Other criteria for a potential donor candidate includes a psychological assessment, a determination of the nature of the donor/recipient relationship, and the underlying motivation for the donor's offer. A former student and friend of both Peg and I then came forward and offered. Again, we waited for approval from Mayo. Again, this was not quick or easy. It took Gretchen more than four months to get final approval.

Then Peg needed final approval, which involved an endoscopic examination of her abdominal area to once again check for any cancer outside the liver.

After both women had been approved, it was on with the game—maybe. The waiting game continued as we waited for a surgery date and tried to keep our patience. Peg was ready, Gretchen was ready, and so we waited.

The scheduled day of surgery finally came and offered new opportunities to practice our patience—waiting for word of the surgery's outcome, waiting for the last postoperative test results, waiting to be released from the hospital, waiting to go home, waiting each week for the latest numbers on Peg's blood draw. Waiting, waiting, waiting.

You would think that after so much practice we would have developed a certain degree of proficiency at this waiting game. It never got easier. Maybe we are just slow learners!

CaringBridge Website
Saturday, December 18, 2004

"Just found this quote for you:
'The friend given to you by circumstances over which
you have no control was God's own gift.'

—Frederick Robertson"

CaringBridge Guest Book
Marie and Dick, Minnesota

As you know, we have a date for the surgery, and
now we have a place to stay postsurgery. Peg and
Gretchen will be at the Gift of Life Transplant House.
The Gift of Life Transplant House is a wonderful facility
available to Mayo pre- and post-transplant patients. Recipients can stay only if they have a full-time caregiver
while the patient is recovering. The house, a beautiful,
old home four blocks from the clinic, is run by the Order
of Saint Francis Sisters. Mennonite women come to do
general housecleaning several times a week. It is a great
alternative to a motel room and a terrific place to stay.

Peg has three wishes; Wish number one is that
Gretchen has a successful surgery and a quick recovery.
Wish number two is the same as wish number one but
for Peg. Wish number three is that she recovers quickly
enough to watch the Packers beat the Vikings.*

The Green Bay Packers from Green Bay, Wisconsin,
and the Minnesota Vikings from Minneapolis are rival
teams that play in the National Football League. You
know you are in Packer Country when the churches
reschedule their services on Christmas Eve to accom-
modate Packer fans (the Green Bay Packers play the
Minnesota Vikings at 2:00 PM on Christmas Eve day).

Some churches will not have services during game time.

Ken

* Apologies to the Minnesota Vikings and their fans. The Vikings have given us much pleasure and pain over the years. Both Peg and I are avid Green Bay Packer fans, and the Vikings are the team we love to hate. I trust that you purple-and-gold aficionados (the Vikings' team colors) can take a joke. As a matter of fact, if you are a Viking fan, I am sure of it.

Peg, John, Ken, and Geri—Packer fans all

CaringBridge Website
Wednesday, December 22, 2004

"Hope is the thing with feathers that perches in the soul
And sings the tunes without words and never stops at all."

— Emily Dickinson

CaringBridge Guest Book
Jo and Terry, Wisconsin

Today is the day ...

Today is the day that Peg will receive the 1,499th liver transplant performed at Mayo Clinic Rochester.

Today is the day that Peg will be the 15th person to receive a liver transplant with her diagnosis, neuroendocrine metastatic cancer.

Today is the day that Peg and Gretchen will become the 36th adult-to-adult liver transplant performed at Mayo since 2000.

Today is the day that Gretchen will give Peg life.

Gretchen's day will start at approximately 5:30 AM. Her surgery will begin at approximately 7:30 AM. She should be "closed up" between 1:00 and 2:00 PM, give or take. Peg's day started last night when they began her preoperative preparations. Her surgery should begin about 9:30 AM and be complete around 1:00 to 2:00 PM.

Our anchor through this whole process has been Chaplain Mary Johnson of the Chaplain Services at Mayo Clinic. She has been with Peg since her initial surgery in October 2001. Our medical doctors, departments, treatments, nurses, etc., have all changed these past three-plus years as the diagnosis and treatment have changed, but Chaplain Johnson has been with us every step of the way. She has truly been a God-sent gift.

Chaplain Johnson presided over a little ceremony last night for Gretchen and Peg, two courageous and beautiful women.

I will update this page today as I get new information. Keep your love, concern, and prayers coming because—today is the day!

4:00 PM: Gretchen is in recovery. Her surgery started at 8:45 AM.

4:30 PM: Peg is in recovery. Her surgery started at 10:45 AM.

10:30 PM: Both Gretchen and Peg are doing really well. Gretchen is somewhat alert and responsive, but drowsy. The same is true for Peg. Both have had some tubes removed, Gretchen more than Peg. Both are in ICU. The doctors are very pleased with their recovery. They both went into this experience in very good physical shape, and that has helped a lot. More tomorrow.

Ken

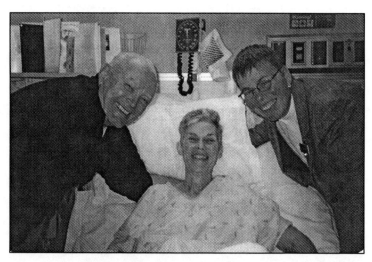

Ken, Peg, and Chaplain Mary Johnson

And How Are You Feeling?

We Must Find Peace…

Even the hurricane is quiet in the eye
Buried ever so deep in its heart the stillness is found
A nucleus that is mysteriously calm.
Engulfed in the hurry, worry, hubbub of our day
When everyone is flying aimlessly in all directions
Try to find a silence of your own.
Discover your personal bit of inner peace
And cherish every minute.

—Tommy Felton
Images—Women in Transition, compiled by Janice Grana

ow are you feeling? How many times have we been asked this question, and how many times have we lied in response? I would guess many times and for many different reasons. Sometimes, I just didn't know what I was feeling. Sometimes, I get the sense that the person asking the question isn't really interested in my answer. At those times, I usually rely on the old standby: "Okay."

Not true, but good enough. Sometimes, I didn't want to share what I was feeling because it would just take too much energy or because I couldn't allow myself to be so vulnerable. Sometimes, I knew what I was feeling but didn't want to share it with the person who was asking. Expressing feelings is often difficult. It takes time and energy, and it also requires understanding one's own feelings.

Feeling is feeling, and thinking is thinking, and never the twain shall meet. I believe that some people think they are feeling, but instead, they are really thinking. I believe some people have a very difficult time recognizing what they are feeling. Thinking is not feeling, and feeling is not thinking. Both involve different processes, and both involve different parts of the body. When I am emotionally "caught up" in a situation, it can be difficult to "think straight." Sometimes when I am asked how I feel about something, I am so "into my head" I can't get in touch with what I feel.

If you ask friends what they are feeling, and they start their response with "I feel like...," I would bet that they are sharing a thought and not a feeling. The same is true for starting the answer with "I feel that ..." You think with your brain. You feel with your body. Your body tells you what you are feeling.

Do you want to know what you are feeling? First, stop thinking, quiet your mind, and focus your attention on what is happening in your body. If you listen to your body, it will tell you what you are feeling. Sometimes your body may be screaming its response in a way that is impossible to ignore. When my fists are drawn tight and my teeth are clenched, I know I am really, really angry. Sometimes my stomach is hurting and my forehead is furrowed and I'm in a cold sweat, and I know I am really, really scared. Try as we might, sometimes we just can't ignore our body's messages. At other times, figuring out what you are feeling is not so easy. The feelings may not be strong, or your body may be sending you mixed and confusing messages. At these times, you need patience and skill to put words to the feelings.

Sharing feelings is a learned communication skill. The process is a step-by-step procedure. Step one is becoming aware of your body's sensations. Step two is staying with the sensations long enough to find a word that best describes that feeling. Step three is sharing these feelings, if you so choose.

In this highly stressful time of Peg's liver transplant process, I realized that expressing my feelings was essential to maintaining my mental health. Had I not been able to do this, my already sky-high stress level would only have increased. And so I shared as best I could. I shared by talking with Peg. I shared with friends. I shared through the CaringBridge website each night. I did all of this because it helped me. I trust that the sharing of my experience might have helped others, too. Talking about my feelings was a mainstay of my emotional health. To do otherwise would be to court disaster.

I am now in the process of learning how to play the guitar. I do not find this easy to do. Getting my fingers in the right position at the right time can be really frustrating, but I practice. I practice each day. My daily progress is negligible, but I see quite a difference when I compare what I could do six months ago with what I can do now, The same is true for learning to express one's feelings.

Talking about feelings takes practice. For some, this may be easy. I believe women open up much better than most men. I also believe that there is a huge benefit to learning this skill. Being able to know what you feel and being able to communicate it can help you reduce stress, which can make a tremendous difference in how you handle the situation.

Sharing feelings with another also helps someone get to know you. This is, in most cases, a good thing. Even more importantly, however, reflecting on your feelings is a great way to get to know yourself. By the very act of disclosing yourself to another, you learn more of who you are. Putting feelings and thoughts into words and expressing yourself is really the pathway to self-knowledge. How many philosophers have urged us to "know thyself"? One way to know thyself is to "share thyself."

And how do I feel? Let me tell you...

CaringBridge Website
Thursday, December 23, 2004

> "Take Time To Enjoy"
> The poster reads and
> I silently agree as
> I hurry to my next
> appointment, already
> thinking about tomorrow...

Tears and Pebbles in my Pockets, by George Betts

One of the liver's most important functions is to help eliminate medications from the body. As you can imagine, both Peg and Gretchen have received numerous medications in the transplant process. Because both Peg and Gretchen now have less liver to do the job, it simply takes longer for the after-effects of the medication to wear off. Peg received about 65 percent of Gretchen's liver. Chaplain Mary Johnson suggested that we call Peg's new liver a "liverette."

Peg is doing very well. Her old liver was huge—about four times its normal size. This was obviously the cause for a great deal of her discomfort and pain in the past. That now is history. Her new liver is functioning very well, and the doctors knew that almost immediately. Apparently, this is not always the case, and some people never survive the transplant because the transplanted liver fails to function.

There is some concern about an artery in her transplanted liver, which they are monitoring closely. We will know more about this as they do more testing. They tell us that Peg's disease, metastatic carcinoid tumors of the liver, occurs in about one in a million cases of liver cancer. I knew I married a woman who was exceptional, but one in a million, that's impressive. She is in good spirits, all smiles, and is concerned about Gretchen. What a gal! What a hero! I will keep you posted.

Problem—12:40 PM. The artery they were watching turns out to be blocked. Our surgeon informed us that this is a very serious complication.

They are going to have to correct the situation. The surgery should last about two hours. Keep sending your love and prayers. Apparently, we are not out of the woods yet. …More later.

Update—3:15 PM. Peg is out of surgery. They found the problem and corrected it, we hope. We will not know for certain until they check it out again tomorrow. If corrected, we go forward. If not, more surgery will be required. The worse-case scenario is if the transplanted liver fails and Peg needs another liver and quickly. If this were to happen, Peg would rise to the top of the transplant list. No MELD score then. Only a case of "do or die." Let's pray that this does not happen.

Dr. Poterucha told us to expect problems and to roll with the punches. We are.

More tomorrow.

Ken

And the Answer Is ...

Live in the present,
Do all the things that need to be done.
Do all the good you can each day.
The future will unfold.

—Peace Pilgrim
A Grateful Heart, edited by M. J. Ryan

Knowledge equals control. Knowledge is participation. Knowledge is power. Knowledge is a way to not be left out. Knowledge directs action. When you first get a diagnosis of cancer, your life changes—forever. One of the main concerns, it seems to me, is the question of control. A disease that is so scary and so out of your control changes you. In this instance, one might choose to take on a victim's role.

I suppose not maintaining control of oneself can be viewed negatively, such as "losing control" and being "out of control." Personally, I do not appreciate being controlled by others or being with people whom I perceive as controlling. Nor do I enjoy the company of folks who always seem to be in control and appear rigid or inflexible. These are all negative aspects of control. There are, however, benefits of being in control, especially in the situation in which we now find ourselves.

The ultimate loss of all control, the loss of everything is, of course, dying, and that is probably the first thought that comes to mind. The second thought probably focuses on survival. What can be done? What is my prognosis? Is there treatment? Is there a chance for a cure? What are my chances? Will I survive? In a life-threatening situation, such as a diagnosis of cancer, I see control as not only a positive attribute but an absolute necessity for survival.

When Peg first received her diagnosis, the emotional impact was devastating. It was an out-of-the-blue, totally unexpected event that shook the foundation of our lives. After living with the aftermath of such an experience, her thoughts and mine turned to, "What can I do now?" This is a question of control. After each attempt at treatment and after each failure, we turned eventually to the question, "What can I do now?" To discover what we could control at these times grew from feelings of helplessness and hopelessness. Trying to figure out what we could do next allowed us to garner our energies and spend them in a way that offered a chance for success. It also helped prevent feelings of victimization. We struggled to maintain control of the situation and put our strategies into action. What can I do when everything feels so out of my control? This is the key question, to which, I believe, there is always an answer.

Sometimes the answer to what we could do was obvious. Try the next treatment. Try the new treatment. Try the clinical trial. Try something to carry you forward and to give you hope. But what happens when all these options run out? What happens when all hope is lost because all options are spent? What do I do then to gain a sense of control? How do I continue?

I so admire Peg for her courage and strength in her battle with her disease.

She never spent much time feeling sorry for herself or agonizing over the "Why me?" question. She and I always seemed to ultimately arrive at a place when the question was not "Why me?" but "What's next? What can I do now given our new reality? This last treatment didn't work, and so where do I go from here?" I can't say that this happened easily or quickly, but it always happened.

The shock and disappointment of a failed treatment attempt would, ultimately, give way to a stronger, more life-inviting stance—the stance of control, the stance of not being a victim.

Control, at times, meant prayer. Control, at times, meant mental imagery or meditation. Control, sometimes, meant choosing not to focus on the negatives, but choosing to focus on something hopeful, something life enhancing. Sometimes this seemed almost impossible, the situation seemed truly hopeless. Those times challenged our strength and our fortitude.

When everything else seemed so out of control, we asked ourselves what things we could control. The answer was in where I directed my thoughts, how I spent my time in my mind. "What I am aware of in the present?" If I could become aware of what I was doing, how I was feeling, or what I was thinking, I could gain control over these seemingly uncontrollable events. I attempted to step away from myself and "see" exactly what I was noticing—see myself in action.

After I could do this, I could direct my thoughts. I was in control. I could choose not to think of scary, frightening things. Instead, I could choose to notice the glorious smell of food cooking in the kitchen; the scintillating sounds of leaves rustling in the breeze; the explosion of flavors in my mouth from biting into a fresh, juicy tomato; the sensuousness of slipping into bed with freshly laundered sheets; or simply my breath moving in and out.

Developing this awareness and learning to direct your thoughts sounds so simple, but at times like these, it can be the most difficult and most important thing to do. Try it.

CaringBridge Website
Friday, December 24, 2004
Christmas Eve

Gretchen is having a more difficult time with her pain management. The doctors are changing her pain medication. Hopefully, this will improve things. She is ready to leave this "joint."

Good news for Peg: The artery repair has worked. So far so good. They will be monitoring this very closely, and it still is a major concern, but things look good at this point. All of her vital signs are excellent, and she will be moved out of ICU today and into her own room.

Happy holidays...and *go Pack!*

Ken

CaringBridge Website
Saturday, December 25, 2004
Happy holidays!

> The rainbow is more beautiful than the
> pot at the end of it, because the rainbow
> is now. And the pot never turns out to be
> quite what I expected.
>
> *Notes to Myself*, by Hugh Prather

All is well. Gretchen is sitting up, looking better, and feeling better. They tell us that she may experience more pain than Peg. This has not been easy for her. She is one brave lady.

Peg is sitting up and had her first meal, chicken broth and Jell-O. Whoopee!

This reminds me of a story. Our Aunt Jessie was in the hospital recovering from cancer surgery. Aunt Jessie hated Jell-O, and guess what they brought her for supper? You guessed it: Jell-O. It went like this:

> Aunt Jessie: "Do you know why they give you Jell-O in the hospital?"
> Us: "No, Jessie, why?"
> Aunt Jessie: "Because they want to get rid of it!"

Good point, Jessie!

Needless to say, we are all happy that Peg's third wish came true. How about them Packers!

The doctors have removed some of Gretchen and Peg's abdominal tubes. They can both move about more freely and are encouraged to do so. Today's goal is to be up and moving. Peg has visited Gretchen twice, first in a wheelchair and then by walking with a podium walker.

A podium walker allows a patient to walk in an upright position while at the same time resting her arms on the chest level surface.

Apparently, Gretchen's recovery will be more difficult than Peg's. Gretchen came in feeling well and healthy, and the surgery knocked her down. Peg will recover more quickly because she came in sick and unhealthy and now feels better, thanks to a new, functioning liver. The surgeons tell us that Peg will recover more quickly from the surgery, and Gretchen will leave the hospital sooner.

In 2003, Mayo performed ninety-nine liver transplants. Eighty-nine have been from deceased donors and ten from living donors. As difficult as it is to get a deceased donor liver, it apparently is ten times more difficult to get a liver from a live donor.

This just shows how very fortunate Peg and I and her family and friends are, and how very brave and committed Gretchen is. The show of love and support from both sides, Gretchen's and Peg's, has been overwhelming and humbling. We can't thank you all enough.

And most of all, how do we adequately thank Gretchen for saving Peg's life? We can't. From the size and condition of Peg's diseased liver, Dr. Julie Heimbach, one of our surgeons, thought Peg had about two months before total liver failure.

What a Christmas! Love to you all.

Ken

CaringBridge Website
Sunday, December 26, 2004

> It's not that "today is the first day of the rest of my life,"
> but that now is all there is of my life.

I Touch the Earth, the Earth Touches Me, by Hugh Prather

Good news. Things continue to improve for both Gretchen and Peg. The team of doctors visits every morning, and that is when we get the latest information on our patients. Gretchen had a very difficult evening last night. She was evaluated and treated, and this morning looks 100 percent better. She made her first trip to visit Peg this morning, which involves a trek from her room to Peg's. It takes about ten minutes and is a very good start. Both Gretchen and Peg have experienced complications that are neither unexpected nor unusual, and all have been correctable so far. These bumps in the road, however, give us all some anxious moments. The surgeons tell us that "things are as good as they can be at this point in time." That, we believe, is the most positive comment we can expect from our surgeons. Peg is on many more medications than Gretchen because of her need for anti-rejection drugs. Her favorite is the dreaded oral bowel medication. This foul-tasting fluid prevents gastric infections. The good news is she has to take this only four times a day for twenty-one days— only seventy-two more doses to go. Needless to say, this is not the highlight of her day.

Ken

I Can Hardly Wait…

Tis this one hour that God has given;
His Now we must obey;
And it will make our earth a heaven
To live today — today.

— Lydia Avery Coonley Ward
A Grateful Heart, edited by M. J. Ryan

Every moment that I am centered in the future I suffer a temporary loss of this life.

I Touch the Earth, the Earth Touches Me, by Hugh Prather

I remember my son getting very excited about an upcoming event — the weekend, summer vacation, a long-awaited trip. I can remember him saying, "Dad, I can hardly wait until…"

Although I appreciated his anticipation, I also was concerned about losing the pleasure of the here and now. It may be fun to think about tomorrow, but what about now? What about today?

I can't tell you how many "I can hardly wait" moments Peg and I have had during her illness. I can hardly wait until we get the results of the latest blood test. I can hardly wait to see if the new treatment regime is working. I can hardly wait until I feel better again. I can hardly wait to get my transplant. "I can hardly wait" can go on forever.

We had to learn a very difficult lesson. While waiting for an uncertain future, we were missing the present. "Live one day at a time" became our mantra. We don't know about tomorrow until tomorrow, but right now, we have today.

Today is a glorious time to be alive. Today is the wonderful time to look into Peg's eyes, see her smile, and appreciate all of her in the here and now. Today is all we have, and it must be savored and consumed—for it is everything. To live life in its fullest each day creates a lifetime of full days. "I can hardly wait" will have to wait. I am too busy living today.

....

CaringBridge Website
Monday, December 27, 2004

Consult not your fears but your hopes and your dreams.
Think not about your frustrations,
but about your unfulfilled potential.
Concern yourself not with what you tried and failed
But with what it is still possible for you to do.

—Pope John XXII

CaringBridge Guestbook
Marie, Minnesota

Sorry this entry has taken so long, but the day has been absolutely filled with tests, consultations, and meetings. Mayo is extremely thorough in taking very good care of its transplant patients. Finally, we got the results of the last test that I was waiting for before reporting. Rest easy. All the news is good.

First, Gretchen. I think we can say that today she has turned the corner. She is looking the best she has since this ordeal began. The swelling she was experiencing with the excess fluid in her body is greatly reduced, and she now looks like Gretchen, rather than a poor blow-up imitation of Gretchen. The sparkle in her eyes has returned, and so has some of her sense of humor, and if you know Gretchen, I use that phrase loosely. The only noticeable thing is a general lack of energy and the need for lots of rest. This is very understandable right now because she is not only recovering from major surgery, but is also busy regrowing her liver. She is doing well and looks really good.

Peg has had a very busy day. She takes, and we counted, twenty-eight medications each day. Some once, some twice, and some four times per day. We are being trained in how to do this effectively and precisely. It is one of the three things we are in direct control of in her recovery, the other two being diet and exercise.

She had two diagnostic tests today. The first one, a cholangiogram, measured how well the bile ducts were operating. There is some leakage, but it's not a major concern and hopefully will heal by itself without any surgical intervention. The second test, and what the doctors called "pivotal," was an ultrasound to observe how the artery repair is doing. This apparently will continue to be a concern for the rest of Peg's life. However, the further away from the surgery she gets, the greater the chance that she will have no problems. The good news that we waited for almost all day was that the artery is functioning well. The surgeon told Peg that she is doing very, very well. More tomorrow.

Ken

CaringBridge Website
Tuesday, December 28, 2004

Each day a little stronger. I think of something a friend used to say. "How do you eat an elephant?
One bite at a time."

> CaringBridge Guestbook
> *Pat, Arizona*

Today is a good day! Both Gretchen and Peg are do-ing well. All reports are very positive. Each woman is up and walking, connected to her IV pole that holds her medications. The doctors are starting to talk about re-leasing them both to the Gift of Life Transplant House. It may be that they just want to get rid of us! I will, of course, let you know as this develops. Jane (Peg's sis-ter), Jo (Gretchen's caregiver), and I are pretty tired, but it is wonderful to see the positive changes in both our patients.

Tomorrow, Peg will have two more tests. One will be a CT scan to determine the extent of new liver growth. The second will be a liver biopsy to see if there is any rejection. In about 30 percent of the cases, rejection ac-tually occurs, but Dr. Poterucha told us not to be scared by the word. If rejection does happen, they can correct it with the appropriate medications.

The challenge for Peg, and especially Gretchen, is to start eating. Food does not taste very good to either one of them right now, and it takes so very little to make them feel full. Liver transplant patients require about one hundred grams of protein each day to repair and rebuild the liver and heal the surgical wounds. Yester-day, Peg ate twenty-seven grams, an increase from the day before. The average person needs about sixty grams daily.

I make copies daily of each comment you send to the guest book, and the highlight of our day is sharing them.

Thanks again for your loving and caring thoughts. More tomorrow.

Ken

P.S. Today is our sixteenth wedding anniversary, and we couldn't ask for a better gift than Gretchen's liver.

....

CaringBridge Website
Wednesday, December 29, 2004

"Peg, keep up the good work! I just got off the phone with Brett Favre (he calls after each game, and I critique his performance). I told him about your situation, and he told me to tell you that, in your honor, he will wear the number 4 on his jersey for the rest of the season."

CaringBridge Guest Book
Jim, Arizona

*Author's note: Brett Favre, the Green Bay Packers quarterback, has worn number 4 since he came to the team in 1992.

Another very good day but also a very long day. Both Gretchen and Peg continue to improve. Both have been relieved of their IV poles and are free to move about.

Mike, our nephew and Jane's son, was here for a week, which was great. He was always ready, willing, and able to do whatever needed to be done. Among other things, the guy is a whiz on the computer, and I really called upon his skills to help me out.

Eldora, Jo's mom, has been here the whole time helping Gretchen and Jo, and cheering for (gasp) the Minnesota Vikings. We tried to console the poor, misguided soul, but she was having a very difficult time (the Packers beat the Vikings), and I feel *sooooo* bad!

Peg is doing really well with her new liver. Actually, it's not a new liver, it's a used liver. Actually, it's not a used liver. It's a preowned, 1957 model with only forty-seven miles on it and driven very gently and mostly to church (i.e., Gretchen was born in 1957 and is forty-seven years old. I don't really know about the church part.).

We got the results of the always pivotal ultrasound test measuring blood flow in the repaired artery, and it was good. We found out that the doctor performing the ultrasound happens to be married to one of our former students. What a small world.

The liver biopsy results will probably not arrive until tomorrow, but as I mentioned earlier, if it is not good, it can be corrected.

More tomorrow.

Ken

....

CaringBridge Website
Thursday, December 30, 2004

"...You now share an experience that can't be told in words, but that you both know through every cell of your body. Perhaps that 'knowingness' will translate to a peaceful acceptance as you work your way into joyful living...in love and gratitude for the mysteries in life."

CaringBridge Guest Book
Barb, Minnesota

Finally, our day is over, and I can get to the computer. This has been a very, very long day, and everyone is exhausted. It has been a day with mixed blessings.

Peg was released from the hospital, but Gretchen was not. Gretchen had a very long and difficult night and a very long and hard day. As you may know, when you go under a general anesthetic, the thing they wait for is for the bowels to start working again. The first indication that this is happening is when the patient flatulates. It may be the only time in your life when you pray for gas. Gretchen is experiencing great difficulty with this and consequently the accumulation of the intestinal gases is causing her severe abdominal pain. We hope that things will improve tomorrow, but it is very difficult to see her hurting and in pain. The doctors are on top of it, and it will be resolved, but it is tough to live through and tough to witness.

The really good news is that in both Peg and Gretchen, the livers are growing. It is hard to believe, but Peg's liver has grown in size by 50 percent and in just one week's time. She is experiencing a mild rejection, and they are treating that with drugs. No one seems to be too concerned. The ultrasound showed good blood flow in the repaired artery, and everything else looks very good. All organ recipients receive immunosuppressant drugs to fight rejection, but the drugs also make the patient extremely vulnerable to other infections.

Peg's day was absolutely filled with consultations, meetings, instructions, and information. We are now more responsible for her recovery. Mayo is always there and ready to help, but the doctors want us to become independent as soon as we can. They obviously feel she is ready. Her recovery continues to be excellent. All those years of healthy living are paying off. We now will go to Mayo almost daily, but on an outpatient basis.

Ken

P.S. Do you know why Iowa does not have a professional football team? Because Minnesota would probably want one!

One Coin...Two Sides

In The Gratitude Journal
of my heart,
your name comes up
again and again...

Hallmark greeting card

Webster's defines gratitude as "a feeling of thankful appreciation for favors or benefits received." Roget's Thesaurus lists synonyms for gratitude such as "thankfulness," "appreciation," or variations of the same. How totally inadequate. How cold and analytical. How academic, and how far from the experience we are feeling. The problem lies not in the accuracy of the definition, but in our inability to put into words the intensity of the actual experience. For us, at this time, the depth of the feelings that accompany the gratitude we feel when our prayers have been answered simply cannot be described adequately in words.

It seems to me that hope and gratitude are two sides of the same coin. You can't have gratitude without first experiencing hope. The opposite, sadly, is not true. Many hope. Many dream dreams and send prayers to the heavens. Many do not have the good fortune to experience gratitude. Who was it that said God answers all prayers and that sometimes his or her answer is no? For us, at this time, the answer was a resounding *yes*. And so now we have the good fortune to feel gratitude.

Hope precedes an anticipated event. Hope is a wished-for outcome. Hope is a wish upon a star. Hope is a buildup of psychic energy. Hope demands effort. Hope is an expenditure of brain waves and molecular electricity that keeps us going and provides a goal. Hope is a building up.

Gratitude happens only after your dreams have come true. Gratitude happens when your prayers have been answered. Gratitude can be experienced only after you have accomplished a goal. Gratitude is a release of energy. Gratitude is a letting go. Gratitude is a profound emotional experience that defies definition, at least at such an intense level when your life has been saved.

So many people helped us each and every day. So many people were kind and considerate and let us receive their positive energy. So many people gave of their skills, their energies, their thoughts and feelings—the health professionals who did their best to save a life; the friends and family who did their best to support us and helped to make the way easier; the person who stepped forward and said yes to being a live donor. She was an angel disguised as a person named Gretchen.

How can anyone else appreciate the intense feelings of gratitude attached to all these people? We cannot. I cannot. It would be difficult for someone else to fully appreciate these feelings of gratitude unless they have had a similar experience.

And so for us now, posttransplant, we have the unbelievable and extraordinary opportunity to experience gratitude. How very fortunate we are.

CaringBridge Website
Friday, December 31, 2004

> Dost thou love life? Then do not squander time, for
> that is the stuff life is made of.

Proverbs for Daily Living,

Great news. Gretchen is *out*! She arrived at the Gift of Life Transplant House this evening. Jo, Laurie, and I picked Gretchen up at Methodist Hospital. Mayo clinic is a complex of buildings which includes two hospitals, Methodist and St. Marys and numerous other facilities. We got back in time to join Peg, Jane, and Mary for the New Year's Eve party at the house. Lots of drinking and dancing and whooping it up, as you can imagine!

Peg went to Methodist Hospital for an IV infusion, an outpatient procedure, which is part of the antirejection regime. The infusion takes about four hours to complete.

We all feel that there is much to celebrate this new year: a new lease on life, a new year, a *happy new year*!

Ken

CaringBridge Website
Saturday, January 1, 2005

Gretchen and Peg look great. We all had lunch together today. It was so nice to see them both sitting up, eating, and talking, just like normal people. We are really glad to be out of the hospital. They took wonderful care of us, and we met some really terrific, caring people, but it is difficult to get any rest there.

The Gift of Life Transplant House is super. It has forty-eight rooms for patients and their caregivers (one cannot stay here without a live-in caregiver), three communal kitchens, four or five dining areas, and many lounges with TVs and books and games. There are also many quiet rooms to read, meditate, or relax. No TVs are allowed in the rooms because they want transplant recipients to move about and socialize, not stay in their rooms watching the boob tube. We have met some really neat people, and we hear the most amazing—and also sad—stories. We all have one thing in common—transplants. Because all of the patients have suppressed immune systems, special precautions must be taken to prevent the spread of infection. No visitors if sick, no flowers or live plants, and no children under the age of eighteen.

Be assured that the Gift of Life Transplant House is a warm and wonderful place to visit, with lots of places and spaces to spend time together. Gretchen will be here a week or so, and Peg most probably a month, give or take. It all depends on how well and how quickly they recover.

Peg continues with her treatment for the mild rejection, which includes special medications and extra diagnostic exams. I will keep you posted as always.

Today, the weather outside was dreary (like the

song), but we were cozy and warm inside. Arizona, where are you when we need you?

More tomorrow.

Ken

P.S. I have two favorite teams—the Packers and any team that plays the Vikings.

Gift of Life Transplant House

Look and Learn, Grandpa

"You gain strength, courage, and confidence by
every experience in which you really
stop to look fear in the face.
…You must do the thing you think you cannot do."

—Eleanor Roosevelt
Bartlett's Familiar Quotations, by John Bartlett

Grandpa John was babysitting his two granddaughters, Alli, four, and Bailey, seven. Grandpa wanted to tape a program on TV, but was having trouble programming the VCR, which I understand is typical for us older folks in this age of technology. Alli, the youngest, after watching Grandpa fumble around with the TV, the VCR, and the remote, went up to him, took the remote from her grandpa's hand, and said, "Look and learn, Grandpa." She proceeded to set up everything for the recording.

Nothing like a life-threatening event makes you look at what is important in life. When your life is put at risk, and you have the good fortune to live long enough to reflect on the experience, I believe we are presented with an opportunity to either "look and learn" or to "run and hide."

Looking and learning takes courage, and it takes wisdom. The looking demands courage. A brush with death is perhaps the scariest thing a person can experience. The question put before us at a time like this is, "Do I look or do I look away?"

Looking means that you allow the scary feelings to arise in your consciousness. You face your fear rather than run from it; you persevere. The looking tells your fear, "Yes, I know you are there, but I am going to see what else is there, too."

The wisdom comes after the looking. It is the "what now" part of the equation. Wisdom allows us to reorder our life's priorities. It attempts to answer the questions, "What is important now? Where do I focus my attention now, and what is a waste of my time?"

Time really is all we have. When the end of life becomes an impending reality, and not just an intellectual possibility, time is the measuring tape. It becomes very precious, and how and where we spend our time becomes the most important thing in life.

There is a story about a man who is chased over a cliff by a mountain lion. He manages to grasp a branch of a small tree on the way down and is able to stop his fall. As he looks around, he sees a bear at the bottom of the cliff, awaiting his arrival. To add to his dilemma, he sees that the branch he is grasping is breaking away from the side of the cliff. At that very moment, he notices a strawberry bush with a beautiful ripe strawberry waiting to be picked. He reaches over, grasps the strawberry, brings it to his lips, tastes it, and exclaims "Oh, how sweet it is!"

We are all dying. Death does indeed define life. Life is life only because it will end someday and become nonlife. "Death" is to "life," as "up" is to "down," or "in" is to "out"—the yin and yang of existence. One defines the other. The question is, in this life, at this time, can I taste the strawberries and exclaim, "Oh, how sweet it is!" It is just a matter of priorities.

....

CaringBridge Website
Sunday, January 2, 2005

"Do you know how to make God laugh? Tell him your plans!"

> CaringBridge Guest Book
> *Dodie, Arizona*

What a time this is. The doctors told us to expect complications, and they were right. First, Peg had to have a second surgery to repair a damaged artery and is now dealing with a mild rejection, which necessitates more trips to the hospital and additional medications. Gretchen, we have learned, had a very serious complication involving her colon, which was unexpected. Had this not happened, Gretchen's recovery apparently would have been easier, still painful, but easier. Both are doing well, but they have little energy. They spend much of each day resting.

Peg's day revolves around her medication schedule. This involves numerous oral medications, in pill and liquid form and injections, administered by yours truly. The medications start at 7 AM and continue throughout the day until 10 PM.

She also has four tubes running from her tummy, which collect body fluids. The fluids drain into plastic bottles and sacks, whose contents have to be measured and emptied regularly. This makes simple things like showering, dressing, and sleeping very difficult and often time-consuming activities. What an ordeal!

Tomorrow, Peg returns to Mayo for yet another liver biopsy that will tell us more about the rejection.

Last night, we had an ice storm. Our car was covered with at least one-half inch of ice that took me forever to clear for the four-block drive to the hospital. I never have to do this in Arizona....

Peg has to be on a low-bacteria diet, which means no fresh fruits or vegetables and no unpasteurized cheese. It's not a big deal, but it does make shopping and cooking a much more serious activity.

Both Gretchen and Peg continue to hang in there. This is not easy, but the payoff couldn't be greater. Two strong and brave women.

More tomorrow. Keep the prayers coming. This ordeal isn't over yet.

Ken

P.S. We actually felt the ground shake here in Rochester after the Vikings lost to the Packers. We understand it was caused by the Viking fans in Minneapolis jumping off the bandwagon. (The Packers beat the Vikings, or did I already mention that?)

CaringBridge Website
Monday, January 3, 2005

A very good day and a very long day. Both Gretchen and Peg visited with the doctors and the posttransplant coordinators, and both received good news. They continue to recover well, and all diagnostic tests to date are good. They have interesting scars on their stomachs. Each has an incision that extends from the breast bone to a point just above the bellybutton and then extends to each side of the body—a sort of inverted peace symbol.

Peg's day started at 8:00 AM, and we didn't return to the Gift of Life Transplant House until 6:15 PM. Gretchen had morning appointments. Peg's biopsy results will be in tomorrow, and we will know something about the rejection then.

A normal liver weighs about three pounds. Peg's diseased liver was almost seven pounds when it was removed. Her pathology report stated that hundreds of tumors were present. We will have a chance to see her liver in the pathology lab later this week. Dr. Julie Heimbach and Chaplain Mary Johnson both encouraged us to do so. Chaplain Johnson suggested that Peg thank her liver for sustaining her as long as it did and then say goodbye. She will. It should be very interesting.

More tomorrow.

Ken

Peg and Gretchen comparing scars

CaringBridge Website
Tuesday, January 4, 2005

Sorry to report that today was a difficult one with mixed results. First, for Peg, the news on the rejection is good. The doctors apparently have solved the problem of liver rejection with medications, but a new problem has been brought to our attention. A bile duct continues to leak and has to be fixed. They will attempt to do this Thursday by an endoscopic procedure called an ERCP that will involve cutting a sphincter muscle going into the small bowel to relieve the pressure on the bile duct. This, the doctors tell us, will allow the bile duct to heal—hopefully. It's not a sure cure, but like everything else in our life right now, it is "wait and see." The Lord must be trying to teach us patience. We want to learn to be patient, but we want to learn it *now*!

Peg will have a 7:00 AM blood draw and another ultrasound tomorrow for another check of the blood flow in the repaired artery. We live from blood test result to blood test result. Today, she was absolutely whipped.

Yesterday was exhausting, and she really didn't have time to recover today with more appointments and procedures while dragging around all the tubes and bottles and bags. She had to undergo some mechanical adjustments to these newly acquired appendages, which corrected some leakage problems, but these were not major procedures—painful and tiring, but nothing major. This experience is like running a marathon. Someday we will be able to look back and "remember when," but right now, it is long and hard, like mile twenty-two of that very long race.

Gretchen had a problem, too. She has developed an infection in part of her surgical site. The doctor had to clean it out and did so without numbing the area—not fun. Not a big problem, but another bump in the road. Jo will have to keep the area clean—not fun.

Gretchen is looking good. It is neat to see Peg and Gretchen interact. They share so much together, which the rest of us can only try to imagine. As difficult as things can get here, from time to time, it is also a magical and spiritual journey. The time will come when this will be a memory.

We read your notes every day. They help us to hang in there.

More tomorrow.

Ken

P.S. St. Peter quizzed three new arrivals in heaven. "What's your IQ?" "210," the first man said. "Lets discuss the theory of relativity tonight." St. Peter turned to the second man. "What's your IQ?" "170," the second man said. "Let's talk about quantum mechanics tomorrow," St. Peter said. He asked the third man, "What's your IQ?" "40," the guy said. "Hey," said St. Peter, "how about those Minnesota Vikings?!"

Caring Bridge Guestbook
Jennifer, Washington

AUTHORS NOTE: Comments about the Minnesota Vikings are made only with loving respect and great affection. I also hope that you realize that all of these comments are completely and totally transferable. Simply insert the name of the team(s) you wish.

CaringBridge Website
Thursday, January 6, 2005

Martin Luther King states "the ultimate measure of a person is not where you stand in moments of comfort and convenience, but where you stand at times of challenge and controversy."

CaringBridge Guestbook
Steph, Wisconsin

Sorry to have missed yesterday's journal entry, but just to add more drama to the situation, I had to make a trip to the emergency room at St. Mary's Hospital last night. A situation came up that I couldn't ignore. I had it checked out, and I am okay. It turned out to be benign vertigo or more simply stated, a case of dizziness without serious medical implications. I spent seven hours in the ER, from 6:00 PM to 1:00 AM, because Rochester had a freezing rain followed by a snowstorm, and many, many people with injuries from falls filled the ER. As you might guess, I didn't have any energy left for writing on CaringBridge. Jane and Kari, a former student who works for the public health department in the Rochester area, kept me company, so I was being attended to by *two* beautiful, young women—not a bad deal! Today I feel better.

Peg and Jane and I have spent another full day at Mayo. The two tests that Peg had came out okay. The ultrasound check of the artery repair continues to be good, and the doctors believe the ERCP done today was successful. We have to wait and see if it produces the desired effect on the bile duct leak. Peg gets two needed days off to rest and recover and begins some blood work on Sunday. She made sure that nothing was scheduled during the Packers-Vikings game! Monday begins what looks like another full week of tests and consultations and patient education.

Yesterday, Peg, Gretchen, Jane, Jo, and I viewed Peg's diseased liver. It is difficult to describe the experience. The liver was massive. It completely filled the tray that the attendant brought to the room. It was sliced up like a loaf of bread, and the liver was absolutely *filled* with tumors. There was so little liver tissue visible that it is a wonder that it continued to function at all. The tumors appeared white, while the liver tissue was dark brown. Each cross section was filled with mostly round, white tumors of every size. There were literally hundreds. The only dark brown areas were the places between the tumors. It was truly an unforgettable sight.

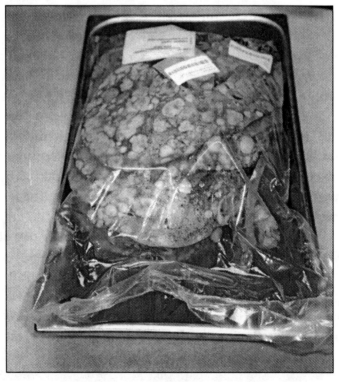

Peg's old liver

Dr. Poterucha said that a person can survive with only 10 percent of the liver functioning. Apparently, the liver is constructed to have plenty of reserve in order to allow it to continue to function effectively even though stressed with disease or chemicals. It is amazing that Peg was able to survive this long.

Being told about the tumors and understanding that the transplant was necessary was one thing, but actually viewing the liver brought the message home as nothing else could have. It was especially important for Peg and Gretchen, as you might imagine. Peg thanked her liver for all that it had done for so long in her life and then said goodbye. This was not a silly, frivolous gesture, but a profound emotional experience.

More tomorrow—I promise.

Ken

A Cool Breeze

All we will have left at the
end of our lives
is
how we have treated each other
and ourselves.

Notes to Each Other, by Hugh Prather and Gayle Prather

One of the rather pleasant and unexpected outcomes of this particularly stressful time in our lives has been the opportunity to experience people's kindness. We have had the very good fortune of being the recipients of the kindness and gentle caring of many people expressed in many different ways.

This kindness may have come with a loving touch or a silent moment of eye contact filled with meaning. It may have come with a card through the mail or an email or a phone call with a query of "How are you?" The words often would hide the highly significant yet unspoken words of "I care about you; I care enough to ask the question."

The kindness that we have experienced is like a sudden, cool breeze on a hot, dry evening—so very pleasant and enjoyable, and so very unexpected.

CaringBridge Website
Friday, January 7, 2005

> We are put on this earth not to see through each other, but to see each other through.

My Journal, Mayo Clinic

Today was a fun day. Both Gretchen and Peg had guests bearing gifts—food, necessities, and fun stuff. It was great to see our friends and to show them around our new home.

The really good news is that Gretchen got her walking papers today. She is a free woman. Hoorah! She plans on spending her weekend here with us and watching lots of football. She will leave for her Eau Claire home on Monday.

Jane (who, by the way, is my favorite sister-in-law) will be leaving Sunday morning. It is difficult to see her go because she was such a terrific help. We have converted her to a Packers fan. She's going to make sure she gets home in time to watch the game. Her son, Mike, I'm sorry to say, is a Steelers fan. The guy lives in Illinois, has terrific relatives who are avid Packers fans, and roots for a team from Pennsylvania—go figure!

They gave Gretchen a neat send-off at Mayo today because it was her final visit. She received a diploma thanking her for her generous gift as an organ donor. Dr. Poterucha, who has been our doctor from the very beginning of this transplant journey, was there and thanked her for saving his patient's life. What a guy.

Let me tell you about Dr. Poterucha. We met him immediately after we left the Mayo Oncology Department for the last time with the very depressing news that there was nothing else they could do for us. We were as emotionally low as we could be. Dr. Poterucha was our next appointment, and he greeted us with, "I like you." We both thought that was strange coming from someone we had not met before.

We learned that he liked Peg as a potential liver transplant recipient. He was the very first person to offer us hope. He was well aware of Peg's condition (he had done his homework in reviewing her medical charts) and was very optimistic for us.

He has been our coordinating physician from the beginning, and we owe him much. He told us early on that the biggest problem we faced was getting a liver. Peg did not qualify for a deceased donor's liver because of her diagnosis. We owe Gretchen for Peg's life, and we owe Dr. Poterucha for making it happen.

All in all, today has been a very good day. Peg gets another day of rest tomorrow, a blood draw on Sunday morning, and then she resumes her week with further testing on Monday. She is really tired from all that happened last week. The doctors tell us that it is very typical to have good days mixed with not-so-good days. She is hanging in there.

More tomorrow.

Ken

P.S. If the Vikings lose the playoff game against the Packers, owner Red McCombs will be looking to sell the team to some investors in the Philippines. The team's new name will be the *Manila Folders*!

P.P.S. Jane is my only sister-in-law!

Peg and Jane

....

CaringBridge Website
Saturday, January 8, 2005

> Yesterday is HISTORY
> Tomorrow is a MYSTERY
> Today is a GIFT
> That's why it's called the 'PRESENT'
>
> (unknown)

CaringBridge Guest Book
Jane, Illinois

A much-needed, quiet day of rest. Gretchen is lookin' good, and Peg is mostly resting and sleeping. Peg is having some pain at the site where the tubes enter her abdomen.

This is a good day to share our experience at Mayo, which has been outstanding. Mayo's philosophy is one of a team approach. It works really well as we have experienced it with our transplant team. The idea that "no one of us is as smart as all of us" is truly put into action here. Remarkable individuals make up our team. The physicians are all called "consultants," a title which reflects their philosophy of working together.

Chaplain Mary Johnson has been with us since Peg's first surgery in October 2001. She has been our friend, our counselor, and our anchor as we have passed through the different programs, departments, and therapies. Aside from her very practical and helpful suggestions to assist us in these tough times, she is always good for a joke. She keeps us laughing.

Dr. John Poterucha, hepatologist and consultant for the Transplant Center, is our guiding light. He coordinates all of Peg's treatments and has been the lifeboat we have clung to as we move forward through this stormy sea of change. A consultant is the highest position of the medical personnel at Mayo Clinic.

Surgeon Julie Heimbach, who as a visiting physician so impressed the Transplant Center staff that they created a position for her, is now a consultant. She was the lead surgeon on Peg's surgery and was absolutely wonderful. She is always straightforward with the facts, always compassionate, and an excellent communicator. A super gal.

Surgeon Charles Rosen, the surgical director, assisted in both Gretchen and Peg's surgeries. He has a twinkle in his eye and a great smile. He and Dr. Heimbach work really well together.

Dr. Tanner oversees the recovery room for transplant patients. He was always there, always helpful, and always smiling.

Pretransplant nurse coordinator Jean Greseth and posttransplant nurse coordinator Kevin Gaustad assisted us with information, relaying messages to the appropriate person and serving as our "on-the-ground" frontline managers.

Nurse Barb Schroeder is a certified healing-touch nurse who has been with Peg at very critical moments to help her relax, focus, and stay centered. She is a wonderful person to have at your side at times like these.

Social worker Jayne Oles is a very helpful person. She connected us with the CaringBridge website and the National Transplant Assistance Fund.

All the nurses in ICU and Methodist Hospital were great, but we had our favorites—Lynnae, Jim, Jane, Jan, Denise, and Carol.

Nutritionists Sara DiCecco and Nicki Francisco told Peg what to eat and what not to eat and answered our many questions. This was not as easy as you might think.

Finally, the many technicians and medical personnel in the various departments have done what was needed when it was needed. A super job done by all.

As you can see, *a team approach*!

We, of course, came here with a team of our own: Gretchen's family and friends and Peg's family and friends. All the cards, the comments on the guest book, the calls, and the prayers have helped us understand how much we are all in this together. Each of you is a much needed and greatly appreciated part of *our team*.

More tomorrow after the Packers game!

Ken

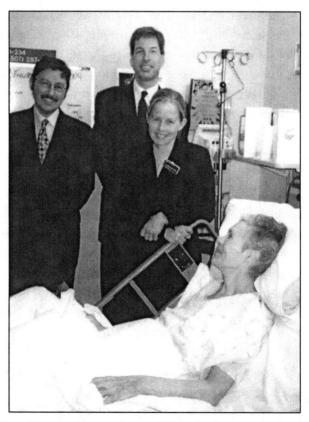

Drs. Tanner, Poterucha, and Heimback at Peg's beside.

CaringBridge Website
Sunday, January 9, 2005

A very good day and a very bad day. Peg and Gretchen had a very good day, and the Packers did not.

Gretchen looks like her old self—oops—I mean her former self, her pretransplant self...you know what I mean. Really, the smile is back, her great, beautiful, shining eyes, and the bright and bushy-tailed look is back. She is excited to go home, but she tells us that it will be difficult to leave, too. We love to see her go, and we hate to see her go.

Peg, also, had a very good day. Not so much pain (except for the Packers game) and feeling stronger. She has a full week ahead of her with tests and educational sessions, and we are looking forward to when they can pull her tubes. This was supposed to happen Tuesday, the twenty-first-day mark, but things have had to be extended because of her complications. Recipients who have a live donor have more potential complications than people who have a deceased donor. The anatomical connections with a partial liver transplant from a live donor are more intricate and difficult than they would be with a complete liver from a deceased donor. We knew all this at the beginning of the journey.

A little story about Jo. Jo is a personal trainer at Gold's Gym in Eau Claire. When we were staying with Geri and John in Eau Claire, I went to Gold's Gym and worked out almost every day. It got me out of the house, and it kept me off the streets—a good thing. People in fitness and physical training have a technical term for the slim, well-defined, and muscular abdomen—the kind you see in fitness magazines and on TV advertising the latest and greatest exercise machine ever invented. They call this high level of fitness and absence of fat on your tummy a "six-pack." Jo, who volunteered to be my personal trainer, set me up with my own program. I told her I wanted a six-pack. She asked if I would settle for a keg! This from *my* own personal trainer.

More tomorrow.

Ken

P.S. I was wondering, what with the Vikings' win over the Packers, if I would have to make another trip to the emergency room for severe gastric disturbance from eating crow!

Student...Teacher...Friend

"My dear friends, I think of you often, every day, several times. I find inspiration in your story because it is filled with love, devotion, understanding, courage, patience, friendship, resolve, and faith. I am in awe of all that you are. I am humbled by your strength and fortitude and love for each other. May you find peace in the healing. Love to you both."

CaringBridge Guest Book
Kari, Minnesota

We have known Gretchen for a long time. Both Peg and I had Gretchen as a student in our undergraduate classes at the University of Wisconsin–La Crosse, and later as a graduate student. I was Gretchen's thesis advisor. Peg also worked with Gretchen's mom professionally.

Gretchen was the type of student who teachers hope to have in their classroom—eager to learn, ready to participate, always asking questions, fun, inquisitive, and intelligent. After her graduation and as she became a teacher herself, we kept in touch, not in a student-to-teacher relationship but one of friend to friend. We were in a book club together. We shared vacation time. We stayed in contact even after we moved to Arizona. We were friends.

To have Gretchen offer to be a donor for Peg was overwhelming. To actually have Gretchen as our live donor is overwhelming. She did this for Peg—for us—as our friend. She tells us we gave her so much as her teachers, and she simply wanted to return what she received, teacher to teacher, friend to friend. Gretchen is more than a friend. She is our hero.

Gretchen and Peg at camp

CaringBridge Website
Monday, January 10, 2005

> The world knows
> very little of its
> greatest heroes.
>
> —Don Ward
> *stronger than cancer,* by Connie Payton

Gretchen and Jo packed up and left today. It was difficult to have them leave. We all cried. It's not like we won't see them again real soon, but it was nice having them next door. We have shared so much. Jo goes back to work, and Gretchen will have some much needed time off to heal and to regain her strength. The doctors say it takes about four months for the donor to feel like herself again. It will take a year for Peg.

Peg's blood draw results were excellent. The blood markers they follow include 36 different components. She gets tomorrow off and returns Wednesday for another full day of testing. We are very hopeful.

Let me tell you about the screening procedures for live liver donors. Since the live liver donor program at Mayo in Rochester started in 2000, eight hundred-plus individuals have volunteered to be a live donor. After initial screenings via telephone, blood tests done locally, and maybe a visit to Mayo for more-invasive testing, Mayo, so far, have accepted—thirty-six live donors—Gretchen and Peg were number thirty-six. Thirty-six out of eight hundred—*wow!* We feel extremely fortunate to have a friend like Gretchen and to actually have had a successful transplant. This obviously does not just happen. It goes like this:

At Mayo in Rochester, the donors have their own pretransplant team, as does the recipient. Each team acts independently of the other to protect its client. Team members do not share information, and decisions are made independently of each other. As a prospective recipient, we never knew what was transpiring with our prospective donor. The only way we found out anything, and that includes who volunteered, was if the donor chose to tell us herself. We also knew that Mayo accepts only family members or friends with whom the recipient has had a long, sustaining relationship. Mayo does not make being a donor easy. And it should not be, because the actual experience is very difficult, and it takes real commitment to see it through.

Gretchen's team had Lisa Bakken, the pretransplant nurse coordinator, and Dr. David Brandhagen, a hepatologist and Gretchen's consultant, among others. I mention these two because they truly advocated for Gretchen to be our donor. The pretransplant team did not make this easy for Gretchen; the process was grueling and exasperating for her at times. We know this because she shared much with us.

All along, we told Gretchen that at any time she could pull out with no explanations needed. Gretchen could have backed out at any time by simply saying she was eliminated, or that it was too difficult, or for any number of other plausible excuses. She obviously did not. The fact that she stayed with the process and stayed with us speaks to the many laudable qualities of Gretchen's character.

Gretchen has long been an advocate for organ donations. She is on the list for bone marrow transplantation; she was even called once but was not a match. She knew that one day she would be an organ donor, but she didn't realize that she would be alive to see it happen. This speaks of her unshakeable commitment to organ donation.

Gretchen hung in there when it would have been very easy to bail out and say that she tried. She did more than try. She was tenacious. She never gave up. She persisted against some formidable obstacles. She persevered. This speaks of her tenacity in acting upon what she truly values.

The true measure of what a person values is not what they say, but what they do, and Gretchen put her money where her mouth is. This act of courage and commitment, driven by what she values, speaks of Gretchen's love of Peg, of life, of giving and sharing in a most profound way. In conversations with Gretchen, she told us, "It just feels right."

Gretchen attended a conference while she was considering being a donor for Peg, and the speaker said, "No matter what the question, love is the answer." That was the clincher for her. No more questions—full speed ahead. Gretchen is our hero. She is our lifesaver. She is love personified. She is our friend. She is very much a part of our lives. She is someone we will love forever.

Ken

All Flies Are Not the Same

"I pray for deep listening in the new century—listening alone—listening together—listening to others—listening to oneself—listening to the earth—listening to the universe—listening to the abundance that is—awakening to and feeling sound and silence as all there is—helping to create an atmosphere of opening for all to be heard, with the understanding that listening is healing. Deep listening in all its variations is infinite. Deep listening is love."

—Pauline Oliveros
Prayers for a Thousand Years,
edited by Elizabeth Roberts and Elias Amidon

So often, what we think we hear and what we think we understand is not exactly what the message's sender intended to communicate. That is one of the many reasons that communicating is so difficult.

One day my son, Karl, came home early from his first-grade class.

Me: You are home early. What's up?

Karl: It's the end of the dime....I mean it's the end of the nickel. ...

Me: You mean it is the end of the quarter?

Karl: Yeah.

My very first job was teaching elementary physical education in New York. I remember one day I was explaining the rules of dodge ball to my third-grade class. The players divide into two teams, and each team tries to eliminate the other team's players by hitting them with a big, soft, red ball. The game has become quite the rage for adults, and a movie has even been made about it.

One of the rules I explained to my class was that if a person catches the ball thrown at him "on the fly," the person who throws it is out. One little boy raised his hand and asked, "Mr. Becker, if I don't catch the ball on my fly (as he moved his hands to the front of his trousers below his belt), but up here (as he moved his hands upward to shoulder level), is he still out?" As I said—all flies are not the same.

Another example of the difficulty of communicating occurred at a friend's house. We were having a very serious discussion and an emotionally difficult time telling our friends about our situation. At a very poignant part of the discussion, our friend's daughter, Cindy, exclaimed, "I bet you cried your balls off!" As you can imagine, that had us all speechless. After all, how do you respond to that? Cindy's mom, however, understanding her daughter better than the rest of us, came to the rescue. She said, "Cindy, do you mean, 'did you bawl your eyes out?'" Cindy replied, "Yes, that's what I mean."

Dime or quarter? Bawl or ball? Fly or fly? What exactly is it that you mean?

Peg and I always saw the doctors, surgeons, and medical staff together. Before our meetings, we always compiled a list of questions to ask them. As the physicians answered the questions, Peg would write down their responses. After the question and answer period, we would have an open discussion regarding Peg's diagnosis and prognosis. At this time I kept notes. We took notes so that we did not have to rely on our memories. It was our attempt at keeping the flies and balls straight. The news we received on many occasions was not good and often was difficult to hear. As one friend told us, when you get nervous, you go deaf. What often happened, which always amazed and confounded us, was that during our discussion together afterwards, what Peg or I heard was not what we had written down. Communication is more than just talking and listening. It is understanding. No easy thing.

CaringBridge Website
Tuesday, January 11, 2005

> Meaning in life can be discovered:
> By doing a deed
> By experiencing a value
> Through suffering
> What matters-above all-is the
> attitude we take-how we accept
> life's circumstances.
>
> —Viktor Frankl
> *Joyful Aging,* by Geri Marr Burdman

Peg had a very good day. She was moving more and had less pain. She had a chest X-ray today and will start with more testing each day for the rest of the week. Nothing will be invasive, but it will be tiring nonetheless.

Back in September 2001, a week after 9/11, we began this journey in the emergency room at Gundersen Lutheran Hospital in La Crosse, Wisconsin. Peg entered with severe pain in her abdominal area that the doctor thought was diverticulitis. As a sort of an afterthought, the emergency room physician decided to do a CT scan. He came back with the news that she had lesions on her liver, told us he thought it was cancer, and admitted her to the hospital that very night. She had a liver biopsy the next day.

We were in shock. We thought they had made a mistake. Peg has always been very health conscious. She has had every screening test possible for cancer and other diseases. She was always concerned about her diet and exercise. She did everything one could do to be healthy.

The biopsy confirmed the initial diagnosis. It was carcinoid cancer. How our lives can change in an instant. We remember when, at first, the doctors all had very somber expressions before the final diagnosis and pathology results were in. On Friday, when the biopsy results were completed, they came in, all smiles, telling us that it was carcinoid cancer and not carcinoma. We were not relieved. What was carcinoid anyway? Why were they relieved?

If it had been carcinoma, Peg would maybe have had six months to live. We were told that carcinoid was a slow-growing cancer. It was also obvious to us—and to their credit, they didn't hide the fact—that they had very little experience with this kind of cancer because it is so very rare.

We saw our physician, Dr. Terman, the following Monday and asked to be referred to Mayo. Within thirty minutes, we walked out of his office with an appointment for the very next day at Rochester Mayo and with all of Peg's medical records.

Dr. Terman said that in his practice of some twenty-five-plus years, he had encountered maybe five or six cases of carcinoid cancer. Our La Crosse surgeon had a similar experience. When we met our physician at Mayo, he told us they see about six or seven such patients each week. This was the place for us!

At first, the diagnosis was a slow-growing, non-functional, carcinoid cancer that had spread to the liver. Peg had surgery, had the primary site in her small intestine removed, and went onto the first treatment phase, the watchful waiting phase.

We were hopeful. If these tumors in her liver were truly slow growing, maybe it was best to do nothing. The doctors guessed she may have had these tumors for ten years or longer. They also estimated that she had multiple tumors, about thirty, that were too widespread to be removed surgically.

The watchful waiting didn't work. The tumors continued to grow and multiply. We then turned to hormonal injections. We were hopeful, but this treatment did not work either.

The tumors were now growing aggressively, so Peg started chemotherapy. For four months, Peg was nauseous, hairless, and without energy. This was a very tough time, but we were hopeful. The chemotherapy did not work. The tumors continued to grow and multiply aggressively.

We then were admitted into a clinical trial with a new drug that showed some promise in cases like Peg's. We were hopeful. The new drug treatment didn't work.

At each stage in this process, we were hopeful. At each stage in this process, we were disappointed and had to regroup.

The final, dreadful news came when we left the oncologist for the last time with the "there is nothing more we can do for you" proclamation. From this lowest of all possible lows, from this dreadful, soul-killing space, from this hopeless place, we walked into Dr. Poterucha's office. You know the story from there.

We now have hope.

More tomorrow.

Ken

....

CaringBridge Website
Wednesday, January 12, 2005

Take time to laugh; it is the music of the soul.

My Journal, Mayo Clinic

A Day in the Life of a Certain Liver Transplant Recipient

7:00 am—Take one pill. Get up and try to get dressed as best you can, given all the apparatuses you have hanging from your body. Also drain and measure the various body fluids that your body has been busy expelling all night long. Shower only if you have lots of time.

8:00 am—Take fifteen pills and one injection delivered in the abdomen by a loving husband.

9:00 am—Take two absolutely disgusting liquid medications, the last of which has to be swished about in your mouth, just so you can appreciate the flavor as fully as possible, and then swallow.

2:00 pm—Repeat the two absolutely disgusting liquid medications.

6:00 pm—Repeat above, lest you forget how absolutely disgusting they taste.

8:00 pm—Take eight pills and one injection delivered in the same abdomen by the same loving husband.

10:00 pm—Lest you forget how absolutely disgusting the two liquid medications are, take them again before you go to bed.

Interspersed between encounters of the medicinal

kind—Go to the clinic and be probed, stuck, injected, and generally made to feel out of control of your own body, which you have thrust into the hands of total strangers.

For your edification, said patient has three bags and two bottles hanging from various areas of her tummy.

A bit of practical advice: The bottles, bags, and tubes do not fit into panties. The best solution is to wear men's boxer shorts provided by one loving husband and then...

Have a nice day!

Ken

P.S. Just to make Peg feel better when she has to wear my underwear, I wear hers...

If I Were You...

A curious thing has happened as we stumbled along this path of uncharted territory, this path of "hope for a cure" and "try the next treatment." The road has been strewn with unsolicited advice.

It is not always prefaced with "If I were you...," but nonetheless, these unspoken words are there.

"If I were you, I would try this treatment. I had a friend, and she did this, and it worked."

"Have you read about this new approach they are trying in (fill in the blank)? It really works."

"I wouldn't trust those (fill in the blank)."

"Have you heard about this place that used only (fill in the blank) methods that really work?"

"Why not go to a hospital that is closer to home?"

At times, you realize that the advice is well-intended and represents the speaker's honest and sincere attempt at helping you. At times.

At times, it is a rude and an unsettling intrusion into your best attempts to deal with a very difficult situation.

At times, it is rather like a smack on the side of the head.

Unsolicited advice, although meant to be helpful, rarely is. It is an accusation that what you are doing is not right. It is an affront to your intelligence and your ability to make good decisions.

This "If I were you…" approach doesn't work because no one else is me. Another person cannot possibly know all that Peg and I have gone through. Another person cannot have the faintest idea of what we have done, what we have thought about, and what we have considered. Another person cannot possibly know all of this, very simply because they have not experienced what we have experienced. Another person cannot possibly put themselves in our position with 100 percent accuracy.

There is a saying about not judging others until you have walked a mile in their moccasins. The same is true for giving advice.

If I can give you a word of unsolicited advice—if I were you, I wouldn't give any unsolicited advice.

Don't Tell Me…Show Me

"May there be such
oneness between you…
When one weeps
the other will taste salt."

—Native American prayer

This is a transplant story, and it is a story about love—so much love by so many people expressed in so many ways. It is hard to know where to begin.

It seems to me that love is much more than an emotion. Certainly, emotions are a part of loving, but only a part. And the emotions involved in loving can be conflicting and disconcerting. I can be angry or disappointed or embarrassed with those I love, but still love them. Indeed, these negative feelings can be aroused only by someone I care about in the first place. If I didn't care, I wouldn't react. The opposite of love is not hate. It is indifference.

But loving demands more than words. Saying "I love you" is not enough. Love ultimately demands action. When I love someone, I pay attention to that person. When I love someone, I tend to that person. I act in loving ways. I notice what is happening with that person, and I respond in appropriate ways. Those I love are important to me—as important as I am to myself. Their satisfaction and security are as vital as my own satisfaction and security. That is love. That is how I know when I love someone. I have to look past the emotions and observe my behavior. This is how I know when someone loves me. Not by what they say, but by what they do.

For me, how I treat the person I love is how I relate to the world. It is a way to be bigger than myself. It is a way to be connected. Loving someone and being loved in return gives each a witness to their existence.

So many people showed us their love in so many ways: the care and support given to us by friends and family; the care and support shown to us by strangers; the professional and supportive care we received from our medical teams. These people were not acting out of a job responsibility or out of a need for recognition. These people displayed their love in how they did their job and how they treated us—not just expertly and skillfully, but compassionately and with loving care.

It has been overwhelming to receive this kind of love from our live donor. It conjures up such deep and passionate feelings that are impossible to express with words or on paper. This person, our Gretchen, put her life at risk to save Peg's. What greater gift can there be than this? What greater display of courage can there be than this? Not only a gift of life for Peg, but a gift to me for saving my best friend. For me, loving my wife gives my life meaning. To be in love and loved by Peg is all that I need. How terrifying to almost lose this and how very joyful not to. And how very close I came.

CaringBridge Website
Thursday, January 13, 2005

Number 1: Yesterday Peg had an ultrasound to check on the repaired artery again, and today we got the news that it is good! This was why she had her second surgery on the day after the transplant surgery. This is terrifically good news.

Number 2: Today she had a test to check on the bile duct leak. The third surgery was to correct the leak, and the leak has healed. Great news.

Number 3: Today she was taken off one of the oral pills and those two absolutely disgusting tasting liquid medications. Wonderful news. Hooray!

The doctors still are watching closely some potential problem areas. Someday this will be over, and we will be able to go home, hopefully in the near future.

It seems to me that our life together, so far, has had three chapters:

Chapter One: Life before Diagnosis

Chapter Two: Life from Diagnosis to Transplant

Chapter Three: Life after Transplant. May this be the best chapter of all!

More tomorrow.

Ken

CaringBridge Website
Friday, January 14, 2005

A long and difficult day. We started at 8:00 AM (at ten below zero) and finally got back to the Gift of Life Transplant House at 5:15 PM. It had warmed up to zero.

Peg had a setback today. Yesterday they told us that the bile duct leak had healed. Today they weren't so sure and ordered another cholangiogram. It showed a small leak...damn! She may have to undergo another ERCP to correct the problem. This is where they insert a tube down her throat and eventually end up at the bile duct where they may insert a stent. We will know more Monday when the doctors get another look at things and decide what, if anything, to do.

Her new liver should be about 90 percent of full size now. It will take about a year to grow to 95 percent. That is simply amazing. Talk about a miracle. It will never grow to be full size, but 95 percent is plenty good when you consider we only need 10 percent of our liver to function effectively.

Peg got her staples out today, about sixty. Her incision looks great. Thank you, Dr. Julie Heimbach. One doctor told us he hadn't seen such a beautiful scar in his ten years of doing this work. He said it is more typical for patients to have some infection or, at the least, an irritation and reaction to the metal staples. Peg's scar was neat and clean.

She continues to carry her bags and bottles. Maybe next week...

Ken

....

CaringBridge Website
Monday, January 17, 2005

> Every morning, everyone in the world receives
> exactly the same gift—a new day.

My Journal, Mayo Clinic

A new week after a hard weekend. Saturday morning Peg woke up with a fever of 100.9 F at 5:00 AM. We have to report anything over 100 F. She had to go into the hospital and get IV antibiotics overnight. Her temperature got as high as 102.4 F before it came down. We were worried, but they released her Sunday, early in the afternoon. They surmised that the cholangiogram caused the fever when pressure from injecting the dye may have forced bacteria into her bloodstream. The next time she needs a cholangiogram, they will give her antibiotics before the procedure.

We had appointments this morning, and all of her blood work looks real good. That means her liver is functioning well. Tomorrow we have the day off, and she has the ERCP scheduled for 11:30 AM on Wednesday. The good news is that after they insert the stents, they can remove the bags and bottles.

The stents will stay in place for six to eight weeks, at which time we will have to return to either have them removed or to have larger stents put in its place.

Peg is doing okay, except she is very tired. The day off tomorrow should help a lot. They told us to expect bumps in the road, but they didn't tell us about the washboard.

After we are finally released, we have to return to Rochester at four months postsurgery (which will be late April), and thereafter yearly from the surgery date.

That will see us in Rochester, Minnesota, every year at Christmastime—give or take. It will offer a nice break from the Arizona heat (temperatures usually run in the sixties and seventies in December, so that is a joke).

Today it warmed up to *zero*, and it felt like a pretty good day. What does that tell you? I remember a particularly hot August in Arizona when the temperatures were about a hundred and five for a week or so. One day, Peg and I were out and about and commented on how cool it felt and wondered if we needed a sweater. It was ninety-six degrees. But it is a dry heat!

More tomorrow. We love to read your comments. It helps us to know we are not in this alone!

Ken

CaringBridge Website
Tuesday, January 18, 2005

> …You don't get to choose how you're
> going to die, or when. You can only decide
> how you're going to live…Now.

> —Joan Baez
> *Joyful Aging,* by Geri Marr Burdman

Peg is doing well. The ERCP is not her idea of a fun activity, so she is a bit anxious about tomorrow. Every time we visit the Transplant Center at Methodist Hospital, the doctor we see is the one on duty that week. We are able to meet with Dr. Poterucha most of the time. I must say that everyone we have met so far has been terrific. This last time we met with Dr. Brandhagen, Gretchen's coordinating physician. Dr. Brandhagen is very impressed with Gretchen. He shared some of what she had to go through to get approved. He said she was quite extraordinary, but we all knew that already.

He told us some interesting statistics. For every one hundred serious, potential live liver donors, about fifty are eliminated early during the interview process for various reasons. Of the remaining fifty potential candidates, about twenty-five are eliminated during the pretransplant physical and psychological testing. Another ten potential donors wind up not going through with the process because their recipients do not survive long enough to receive the transplant. That leaves fifteen of the original group of one hundred potential donors to actually go through the liver donation surgery. So our Gretchen is in a special group of the 15 percent who get to make a live donation.

Gretchen visited her school yesterday and saw some

of her students and fellow teachers. She said that nobody expected her to appear so soon, and the kids were excited to see her. I bet she received a hero's welcome. After about one-and-one-half hours, she was pooped. It will take time to fully recover.

This has obviously been an extraordinary experience that I have tried to share with you as best I can. The intensity of the days and hours and minutes is difficult to communicate because, most times, words do not match the experience very well. Let me give you an example.

Peg had a certified healing-touch nurse who met with her before each surgery. Just before the actual transplant surgery, she gave Peg and me each a small, red velour heart. It was soft and squeezable. She said a little prayer over Peg as we held the velour hearts to our hearts, asked us to kiss the hearts, and then exchange our hearts. I put Peg's in her hospital sock so she knew she would have it with her during the surgery. Mine I kept and squeezed often during her surgery.

This may sound simple and not very profound, but I cannot recall this experience without it bringing tears to my eyes. It was a very effective way to help us feel connected when we were apart at such a stressful time.

Most days have something that happens that, in light of the reality of our life right now, seems filled with meaning. To live with dying as an ever-present potential is to live life more fully, more consciously, and more purposefully. I cannot speak for Peg, but in some ways, I have never felt more alive.

More tomorrow after the ERCP.

Ken

CaringBridge Website
Wednesday, January 19, 2005

"Just about every time I read each new entry in this fascinating journal, I'm reminded of a favorite childhood book that my grandmother used to read to me, *The Little Engine That Could*. It was never read to me without a follow-up discussion of the 'I think I can' philosophy (in a child's context...but it sure applies to adult lives because we want to always move forward, keep trying, and never give up). Life is full of mountains and blooming prairies. This particular mountain is a bit more than anyone needs...but I know you can do it because you know you can, too!"

> CaringBridge Guest Book
> *Julie, Wisconsin*

The day started at 7:20 AM with a blood draw. We then returned at 11:30 AM to get Peg prepped for another ERCP to check the bile duct funtion in her liver. The actual procedure took about two-and-one-half hours, which is longer than usual, but it was more technically difficult because of the live donor transplant as compared with a deceased donor's complete liver. Two stents were placed in the bile ducts to help them heal and to keep them open. The doctor said everything went well, but we meet with our surgeon tomorrow to get the actual results. We returned to the Transplant House at about 6:45 PM. Another long day.

Those of us "in the know" know that ERCP stands for endoscopic retrograde cholangiopancreatography. Say that three times without stumbling, and receive one free!

In the past week Peg has had:

— a chest X-ray

— a renal clearance test to make certain that the medications have not damaged her kidneys

— an ultrasound (or what those of us "in the know" refer to as the "jelly on the belly" test) to check on the repaired artery

— two cholangiograms (Thursday and Friday) to check on the bile ducts. These tests are the reason for the tubes and bottles.

Interspersed between these tests have been numerous blood draws, an education program for post-transplant care and feeding of your new liver, and consultations with our coordinating physician, the surgeon, the nurse coordinator, and the dietician. And you thought you had a busy week!

Today, by the way, we had a heat wave. The temperature rose to 20 degrees above zero, and silly me—I forgot to bring my shorts.

More tomorrow.

Ken

....

CaringBridge Website
Thursday, January 20, 2005

So far Peg is doing well. That's the best they could tell us today. That also means we are still waiting to get the tubes and bottles and bags removed. Keeping these in place allows easy access to Peg's liver for X-rays and also allows an easy visual check on the fluids being excreted. The doctors tell us that it is easier to keep them in place than to take them out too early and have to reinsert them later. This apparently is something you don't want to do. Aside from lugging all that apparatus around all day, the painful part is where the tubes actually enter Peg's tummy. If they get pulled or if she sits wrong or if they get bumped, it hurts. It is a constant source of irritation. She can't wait until they are out.

Today she was so dehydrated that she had to get IV fluids, which meant three hours attached to a bag in the infusion clinic. This was a direct result of the ERCP procedure yesterday. We started the day at 11:30 AM and left the clinic at 5:30 PM. The lack of fluids made Peg feel lightheaded and weak. It just seems to go on and on.

She had visitors (Gretchen, Jo, Geri, and Rose), and we all had some good laughs—a lot at my expense, I might add. If you know Rose and Doug, you might ask them what they brought. I am too much of a gentleman to mention it here.

So many good and positive things continue to surround us. The day of Peg and Gretchen's surgeries, the waiting room was filled with friends and family from both sides. One of Geri and John's daughters, Kelly, is a massage therapist. She showed up with her special massage chair and gave everybody a massage. It provided a wonderful break from the tension of the waiting and worrying. If you weren't there, you missed a good thing. She had nurses and strangers lining up to get a freebie. I had to beat them off with a stick. Thanks again, Kelly.

Peg gets tomorrow and Saturday off, so she will have a chance to rest and recover.

Later.

Ken

Kelly and her massage chair

CaringBridge Website
Friday, January 21, 2005

> Give me a sense of humor,
> Give me the grace to see a joke,
> To get some pleasure out of life
> And pass it on to other folk.
>
> —Anonymous
> *A Grateful Heart, edited by M. J. Ryan*

Warning: *X-rated*! Do not let your children read this!

Okay, okay. I have had so many inquiries about the gift from Rose and Doug that I feel compelled, almost forced, to share it with you. My reluctance only comes from my effort to protect Rose and Doug (I really think it was Rose's idea).

Rose brought a bag of goodies—coffee, tea, candy, crackers—neat stuff. But the item that shocked me, if you can believe it, was a calendar. This was not any old calendar, but (yikes!) a Playboy calendar. Now, I normally never look at things like this, but it was a gift, and I really need a calendar, and I didn't want to disappoint Rose and the gift she so lovingly gave me, so...we all looked at the calendar.

It started with January, followed by February, and so on. Now, usually after a while, one gets bored—you know—"ya seen one, ya seen 'em all" kind of thing.

However, the pictures included additional remarks and diagrams. These, I assure you, were not part of the original photographs. Rose or Geri or Gretchen or Jo—or who knows who—had defaced these pieces of art with their own drawings and comments. Many of the women had scars on their abdomens. The scars were an inverted "Y" that extended down from the sternum (between the goal posts, if you know what I mean) to just above the belly button and then down to each side. They looked exactly, and I mean *exactly*, like the scars on Gretchen and Peg. I never knew that liver transplantation was such a common thing. Ms. August had a particularly beautiful scar.

I hope I haven't offended anyone with this entry, and I only shared it with you because of the anxiety I caused by my comments about yesterday. Rose seems like such a nice lady, too!

Oh, Peg had a really good day!

More tomorrow.

Ken

Rose's gift

Fun times at camp

CaringBridge Website
Saturday, January 22, 2005

True Story number one:

Upon learning that her sixth-grade son needed proper attire for his physical education class, Mom called the local department store.

Clerk: Hello?

Mom: Hello, my son needs gym clothes. Do you sell jock straps?

Clerk: Yes, ma'am, we do.

Mom: Would you hold one for me? I will come and pick it up later.

Clerk: Certainly. What size would you like?

Mom: Size?…Size?…I guess about an inch.

Humor is good for you. Laughing is good for your body and soul. Laughing is fun. I believe we could all laugh more, unless you have just had a liver transplant. In that case, laughing hurts. Sometimes in the midst of a serious situation, something happens that is hilarious but occurs when it would be most inappropriate to re-act—to laugh. Someone within Mayo, who shall remain unnamed, told me about two real-life incidents:

True story number two:

A woman was just told that her husband had suffered a myocardial infarction (a heart attack). She called to tell the others, and in response to the obvious question "what happened?" she replied, and I quote, "I don't

know. They told me he had a massive internal fart!"
Sounds horrible.

Don't laugh!

True story number three:

A husband was explaining what had happened to his
wife, who had just been in a serious car accident. As he
held his hand to the center of his chest, he explained
that the steering wheel "hit her right in the middle of
her scrotum!" I bet he meant to say sternum.

Don't laugh!

One of the things you do as you grow older is tell
others the specifics of your ailments, and of course, others, given the opportunity, will return the favor. One
upside to our experience is that Peg and I have a lot of
material that we can now share with others.

To give you an example of this black humor, we have
a friend in Arizona who tends to have a lot of colonosco-
pies. I won't mention his name, but you know who you
are, Ted. Anyway, one of the fun things we do when a
group of us gets together is to place bets on how many
polyps this person will have at his next colonoscopy.

Don't tell me we don't know how to have fun!

Peg had another good day. She will have another
blood draw tomorrow at 7:00 AM, and then we plan on
watching the football games in the afternoon. It is not
the same without the Packers, but just wait until next
year. Because of all the surgery on her abdominal area,
Peg can't sit upright for very long, so she has to be in a
recliner. She can only sleep in a recliner also, and that
is getting to be tough on her back. She can't lay on her
side, and certainly not on her stomach. She has a really
difficult time finding a comfortable position.

We meet with the doctor Monday to get more information on the effectiveness of the stents and, of course, her blood work. She is looking good!

Take care and laugh more!

Ken

CaringBridge Website
Sunday, January 23, 2005

Not much to report today. Peg had a blood draw this morning at 7:00. The lab is open 24/7, and this morning it was busy.

Each day the population changes at the Gift of Life Transplant House. People complete their treatments and leave, some new folks enter to begin their journey, and some are here for a checkup. Empty rooms are unusual. I can't imagine how difficult this would be if we had to stay in a motel.

On several evenings, all the residents have been treated to free meals. On Christmas Day, we had a buffet supplied by a local restaurant, The Canadian Honker. One night the local girls' hockey team hosted a barbecue meal from Famous Dave's. Another night, a women's group brought homemade soups for everyone. Tonight we had roast turkey supplied by the House and cooked by the residents. In all ways, this is a wonderful place to stay.

After you are admitted, you can stay as long as you need to. A couple from Mexico City were here five months waiting for a liver transplant. Another couple just came yesterday from Anchorage, Alaska, while he waits for a heart transplant. He is in immediate need but is waiting for an appropriate match. They are probably in their twenties. Another man had a heart transplant fourteen years ago and is now back for a kidney transplant. The rejection drugs he was taking for his heart destroyed his kidneys. There are many kidney and stem-cell recipients.

Some folks are beginning their journey, some are in the middle, and some are at the end. The residents have to take care of themselves. That means the live-in, full-time caregiver cooks, cleans, does the laundry, and takes out the garbage. There are very few restrictions. All in all, it's a terrific option for transplant patients.

Peg had a very good day today. She is feeling good but still carrying around those attachments. It is the first day of her second month since the surgery. We are anxiously awaiting our meetings tomorrow with the doctors. Still hanging in there.

Ken

....

CaringBridge Website
Monday, January 24, 2005

"Long ago, I read that in heaven you could see individual prayers beaming up like rays of light as people prayed for each other on earth. Know that there are so many beams of prayer for you each as you work through this ordeal that it must be blinding in heaven..."

CaringBridge Guest Book
John and Lori, Minnesota

Good news all around, as far as it goes. The blood work was excellent. The secretions from the tubes look good. No date was set for the withdrawal of the tubes, but we believe it will be soon. The next blood draw is on Wednesday, and we see the doctors again on Thursday.

Today is one month and two days past Gretchen and Peg's surgeries. I thought this would be a good time to share our experience on that day, December 22. I didn't have a chance to see Gretchen beforehand (she went in very early), so my comments are limited to what I observed with Peg.

Early in the disease process, Peg worked diligently in maintaining a positive attitude. Each day, usually in the morning, she would have a quiet time where she would pray, meditate, and read. Most often she would have soothing, relaxing music playing. She spent this time focusing on staying positive, using visualization to see everything going well and to stay calm, peaceful, and centered. This was an absolutely necessary part of her day, and when she missed doing this, her day typically was more difficult.

When faced with life-and-death issues that appear to have no simple or easy solutions, or even no solution at all, often we spend our time on negative and depressing thoughts. This does not help. The situation may be out of your control, but what you choose to think about is not. Your thoughts may be the only thing you have control over at a time like this. Saying this is easy— doing it is difficult.

During this time, the most obvious symptoms of Peg's progressing illness were tumor fevers, increasing pain and discomfort in her abdominal area, and an increasing loss of energy. She was tired all the time. We had to plan our day around one activity and only one activity. That was all she could handle, and it was something to look forward to each day. As her liver failed and the tumors grew and multiplied, her facial skin color changed too. She looked gray and sallow and drawn. The disease was obviously taking its toll.

Now, they have done some research on the power of prayer. They have had patients matched as to disease, severity, and other markers to try to have each group be as similar as possible. One group, selected randomly, was prayed for without their knowledge, and the other matched group was not, also without their knowledge. This is typically how research is done so scientists can try to determine if a particular factor, in this case prayer, makes any difference.

In some studies, prayer made a difference. The prayed-over group experienced fewer fatalities, had fewer complications, and recovered more quickly in a statistically significant way.

Now this I know. On the day of Peg's surgery and before receiving any medication, Peg looked absolutely beautiful. Her face glowed with a rich, healthy pink that I had not seen on her for some time. Her cheeks were rosy. She appeared very calm, relaxed, and very much at peace. All this just before being wheeled away to the operating room. I was not the only one to observe this. Others who were with her at this time can testify to what they saw. Chaplain Mary Johnson said that Peg looked "radiant."

Many people were praying for Gretchen and Peg that day. Many people we knew and many we did not. As far as we are aware, we had prayers said in Arizona, Wisconsin, Illinois, Minnesota, California, Washington, Ohio, New York, Montana, Florida, Oregon, Georgia, British Columbia, and even Australia. We believe it made a difference. I know I saw a difference.

Thank you all!

Ken

You Play the Hand You're Dealt

"It seems that Life drops many bags of gold in our path. Rarely do they look like what they are. I ask my patient if Life has ever dropped him a bag of gold that he has recognized and used to enrich his life. He smiles at me. 'Cancer,' he says simply. 'I thought you'd guess.'"

Kitchen Table Wisdom by Rachel Naomi Remen, M.D.

Peg and I play bridge. It is a fascinating and complex game. Each hand is different and you not only have to decide which card to play but your opponent is always there trying their best to defeat your contract. The contract in bridge is the goal you strive to achieve in playing the hand. You never get to choose the cards you hold but you play the hand that you are dealt.

The same is true in life. There is much in life that you don't get to choose, you do the best you can and there are many opponents that can make life difficult. You only get to play the cards you are dealt. Peg and I never felt angry as to how the cards were dealt. It doesn't make much sense or help to get angry at the dealer. It's really just the way the cards fall. Peg nor I ever got angry at Mother/Father God for our situation. We were often sad or depressed. We, at times, felt helpless and, at times, felt hopeful. Sometimes it took a while to decide what to do but we never gave up and we do the best we can—together—as partners.

I am a deeply spiritual person as is Peg. I believe there is much more to life than we will ever be able to understand. That is why it is called the "mystery" of life. Trying to understand what life is all about is like trying to truly understand the idea of infinity. I cannot wrap my mind around the concept of a universe without end—infinite. Everything I have ever experienced in life is finite. Everything has a beginning and an end. Everything has its edges. Intellectually, I can see that infinity is true but it is very difficult for me to understand it fully and completely. For me, the same is true about spirituality. I believe there is more to life than I will ever be able to understand. I believe there is a higher power whose motivation and methods are beyond my grasp. I pray for what I need and want. I hope for the best. I do the best I can. I believe that there is a God that I will someday come to understand, but it will not be in this lifetime.

Many "bags of gold" have been strewn in our path on this transplant journey: Gretchen, Mayo Clinic, Dr. Poterucha, Chaplain Mary Johnson, family, friends, healing, survival, the love that Peg and I share. All miracles. All beyond my control and understanding. I play the cards I am dealt for there is much going on here that I do not completely understand. I trust that someday it will all make sense. I truly believe that it will.

In the book *tuesdays with Morrie* by Mitch Albom, Morrie shares this story. "…The story is about a little wave, bobbing along in the ocean, having a grand old time. He's enjoying the wind and the fresh air-until he notices the other waves in front of him crashing against the shore. 'My God, this is terrible,' the wave says. 'Look what's going to happen to me!' Then along comes another wave. It sees the first wave, looking grim, and it says to him, 'Why do you look so sad?'

The first wave says 'You don't understand! We're all going to crash! All of us waves are going to be nothing! Isn't it terrible?' The second wave says, 'No, *you don't understand*. You're not a wave, you're part of the ocean.'"

CaringBridge Website
Wednesday, January 26, 2005

"To pray is to pay attention to something or someone other than oneself. Whenever a man so concentrates his attention—on a landscape, a poem, a geometrical problem, an idol, or the True God—that he completely forgets his own ego and desires, he is praying…"

Oregon Quarterly, Autumn 2005, taken
from *A Certain World* by W. H. Auden.

Sorry to have missed last night's entry. The computers were down. These things are great when they work, but when they don't, #$%^&*!

One thing one has to learn here, and quickly, is to hang loose. For instance: On Monday we thought we had appointments for a blood draw on Wednesday and a meeting with our nurse coordinator and Dr. Poterucha on Thursday. We got a call Tuesday afternoon that we had an appointment added for this morning at 10:00 AM with our surgeon, Dr. Rosen.

The good news is he removed two tubes, two bottles, and two bags. Peg now has only one remaining tube and bag, and that is to drain bile fluid. Hopefully, this will be removed soon and she will become bagless. Yea!

The Transplant Center at Mayo (Station 10-A) is always busy. They see all types of transplant patients here—liver, pancreas, kidney, and stem cells. Heart transplant people go somewhere else. We see people at all stages in this process. We have gotten to know many of them at the Gift of Life House.

I must say that all of the Mayo staff who have worked with us have been very professional and courteous. They have never given us the impression that they would rather be somewhere else or that we are really a bother. We, of course, have our favorites, but everyone has been super.

An example of their interest and dedication is after Peg's second surgery, both of our surgeons, Drs. Heimbach and Rosen, had the day off. It was Christmas Day. Both Dr. Heimbach and Dr. Rosen came in to check on Peg at different times. They sort of just showed up. Both told us "not to tell anyone" —so don't tell anybody. They obviously care about their patients, and it shows.

I will keep you informed as long as the "#$%^&* computers are working.

More tomorrow.

Ken

P.S. I forgot two states in yesterday's entry—New Mexico and Alaska. I think that's the first mistake I made this year!

....

CaringBridge Website
Thursday, January 27, 2005

> "Thinking of your return for me is great.
> Yet I understand that you hesitate.
> Being weaned is never fun—
> until after it is done!"

CaringBridge Guest Book
Serene, Arizona

A visit with Dr. Rosen, our surgeon and a compassionate and gentle man, and presto change-o! The last bag is gone. This bag was attached to Peg's leg. The two bottles were safety-pinned to her shirt, and the other two bags were attached to the sides of her abdomen. As you can see, she had a lot of excess baggage. What a relief to have them gone.

The bile tube has to stay in place until our return visit (the beginning of March). This tube gives us feedback on the bile duct's functioning, so once again, they are being very cautious, and that is fine with us. It is the smallest of all the tubes, and we don't expect it to be too troublesome.

It looks like they are ready to give Peg her walking papers. We have another blood draw on Sunday morning and a visit with the surgeons Monday. We should get the final word then. They tell us that everything looks very good. After all Peg has been through, hearing this is wonderful. We are certain that they wouldn't release her without everything checking out A-OK.

It is strange to contemplate leaving Rochester and Mayo. On one hand, we are excited about finally being able to go home, and yet it is a little scary to leave the security this place now represents for us. Arizona is not exactly around the corner, but we know the danger signs to watch out for and what to do if they happen. Peg was in such good health before this all happened, so we are very optimistic about our posttransplant life.

We visited Dr. Pitot, our oncologist, today. He was the physician who treated Peg's cancer until it was obvious that nothing more could be done and a transplant was Peg's only hope. It was great to see him, fill him in on the news, and thank him for all his efforts. Like most of the doctors we have had the good fortune to have, a very gentle soul.

More tomorrow.

Ken

....

CaringBridge Website
Friday, January 28, 2005

> "....God's healing is in the love of family, the compassion of friends, the selfless act of complete strangers. God's healing is the strength that lies within us, the courage to fight, the determination to prevail against overwhelming odds. God's healing is at work when we overcome our fears, when we reach out to help one another, when we refuse to give in to despair.
>
> *Talking to God* by Naomi Levy

A rather slow and restful day. No tests or exams. Just healing and recovering.

Both Gretchen and Peg are experiencing abdominal pains today. We think Peg's pain is from the tubes being pulled. I can't believe how much of the tubes extended into her tummy. At first, Dr. Rosen was just going to "crack" them, which means to move them a little as a prelude to their removal. After he got started, he decided to take them all the way out—not a walk in the park. These tubes are normally left in for twenty-one days. Peg's were in for thirty-six days because of the difficulties encountered with a live, partial liver transplant as compared to receiving a deceased complete liver.

As Peg progresses, her medications are reduced. She now takes eighteen pills a day. This will continue to lessen until a time when she may only be on one antirejection drug. This could take up to a year. In every case, it is an individual decision based on the person's acceptance of the transplanted liver. After we leave here, Peg will have a weekly blood draw that will be reviewed by Mayo. Based on her blood tests, they will alter her medications. They really have this stuff down. We have no question that we are in the right place.

Gretchen's abdominal pain may be from her over-doing her exercise program. She has an appointment at Mayo on Thursday. We are guessing that the abdominal pains might also be a result of the nerves in the surgical sites "waking up." We really don't know, but it is strange that both Gretchen and Peg are having similar pains at the same time.

Peg is getting out and about more each day. Yesterday she climbed stairs for the first time. Today I took her shopping at HyVee's grocery store, and we drove through a carwash together. Don't tell me I don't know how to show my woman a good time.

Ken

What Do We Do Now?

He who has not looked
on Sorrow will never see Joy.

Patterns of Happiness, by Kahlil Gibran

As we have progressed along this transplant journey, we have been blessed and overwhelmed with the loving support we have received from our family and our family of friends. We have been treated with kindness, goodness, generosity, and laughter. Peg and I have shared intimate conversation about our love and concern with each other that most probably would not have been shared otherwise. When you have forever, thoughts and feelings such as these often do not get expressed. When our time together may be short, sharing these feelings becomes urgent, and rightly so.

A very sad and unforeseen development has happened to us along the way of this transplant journey. Some of the people who supported us and prayed for us and were there for us have themselves fallen seriously ill or even died. Gretchen's coordinating physician was tragically killed in an automobile accident at age forty-one. Dr. Brandhagen supported Gretchen in her quest to be Peg's donor. I can honestly say that if it were not for Dr. Brandhagen, Peg would not be alive today. Dr. Brandha-gen is no longer with us.

Our good friend David, who was there for us when we were in need, died at age fifty-nine of a heart attack. Our good friend Mary Lynn is fighting lung cancer. She was there for us, and now it is our turn to be there for her. What a strange and tragic turn of events. What an unsettling time.

How do we accept our good fortune and live with the tragic fortune of others, others who were there for us? Right now, we cannot find a suitable answer. Right now, we are saddened by life's uncertainties. Right now, we are overwhelmed with the mystery of it all.

···

CaringBridge Website
Saturday, January 29, 2005

I'm not sure what words to use to describe our feelings about the paradox of our present reality. There just
seems to be such an incomprehensible difference between the community Peg and I find ourselves in now
in Rochester, Minnesota, and what we see on the world
news regarding the situation in Iraq.

In Iraq, it is obvious that many people are dedicated
to death and destruction. Some willingly take their own
lives and attempt to kill as many others as they can in
their acts of suicide and homicide. Their hatred of others or their dedication to their cause is the most powerful motivating force in their lives. They are driven to kill
and destroy as much and as often as they can so they
can cause the greatest amount of pain and suffering and
misery. How can life be so cheap and so expendable?
How can life be such a miserable experience that death
looks like an attractive choice? It is difficult to understand this world.

Right now at Mayo and in the Gift of Life Transplant House, we are living with and being treated by
people who are dedicated to extending life and to human survival. So many skilled and gifted professional
people spend their hours, days, weeks—indeed their
lives—trying to prolong life for others. The residents
at the Gift of Life Transplant House are being given a
second chance at life and trying desperately to survive.
For most recipients, this represents their last chance for
survival, and they are struggling each day for yet one
more day.

All this is done at great expense emotionally, physically, and financially. At this time and at this place, so
much effort is being expended to the saving of life, one

life at a time. Life here is focused on loving and caring for each other. Life here is so very fragile and so very precious.

What a confusing and bewildering difference in the realities between our world here in Minnesota and the world of pain and suffering and hatred we now see in Iraq. What a world!

Ken

CaringBridge Website
Sunday, January 30, 2005

Not much to report today. Peg was moving a little slower, and Gretchen wasn't feeling too good either. We had planned to catch a movie today (a step up from a carwash), but Peg wasn't up to it, so maybe next week. We will meet with the surgeon tomorrow and expect to be released. I will fill you in when we know something new.

Take care.

Ken

CaringBridge Website
Monday, January 31, 2005

Peg got the "okay to go" today. Everything looks good. Tomorrow they will do one more ultrasound before we leave. We fly back to Arizona on Sunday. Since the transplant, much has been lost, thankfully, and much has been gained, thankfully.

Lost are the tumor fevers. These fevers were caused by Peg's body fighting the carcinoid tumors in her liver. The tumor fevers caused her body temperature to rise as high as 102 degrees F. and were accompanied with a total lack of energy. Peg would get these fevers irregularly and without warning. Sometimes they would last three or four days. Once last summer, they continued for three weeks, and I was afraid we might lose her. There was nothing to do, according to our oncologist, but to take Aleve. This felt like trying to protect oneself in a hurricane with an umbrella.

Because of Gretchen, we have gained a watchful eye on Peg's temperature. Now a fever may indicate an early sign of rejection or an infection, both to be taken seriously and both very treatable. We take her temperature two times each day, morning and evening.

Lost is the fatigue caused by the carcinoid cancer. In the past, Peg's decreasing energy level was caused by her body's response to the continual tumor growth.

Now, because of Gretchen, we have gained a fatigue caused by Peg's body recovering from the surgeries and the energy it needs to heal and to grow a new liver—an excellent trade.

Lost is a sixty-four-year-old liver filled with hundreds of tumors. It served her well and must be appreciated for what it accomplished, but it had little time left.

Gained, because of Gretchen, is a new liver, free of tumors and with great potential.

Lost is the anxiety of waiting for a successful treatment. Lost is the dreaded thought of a short and certain future.

Because of Gretchen, we have gained new possibilities with the anticipation of years, not months.

Lost is the uncertainty and the almost unbearable waiting for a successful treatment, a suitable donor.

With Gretchen, we have gained a second chance at life.

Lost is a life filled with fear and dark shadows.

Gained is a life filled with light and a promise of a future.

All this because of Gretchen.

Ken

CaringBridge Website
Thursday, February 3, 2005

We have left the Gift of Life Transplant House in Rochester and now are in our friends' home in Eau Claire, Wisconsin. Tomorrow we leave Grandma Geri and Grandpa John to spend Saturday with our friend Barb in Minneapolis. We fly home Sunday. We have to return to Mayo in three weeks for a follow-up checkup, and if all looks good, we return once a year thereafter.

Leaving the Gift of Life Transplant House was a mixed blessing. On the one hand, we are excited to get on with the rest of our lives, but on the other hand, this place has and will always have a special place in our hearts. Aside from the miracle we experienced here, we have made special friendships with people who have shared a similar time in their own lives. I know we will see some of these folks again. Most we will not. For most, a return here involves an annual evaluation. For some, it means that there is trouble, and more medical intervention is needed. I believe this is the first time in my life that I have said goodbye to someone by saying, "And I hope I don't see you again."

Our transplant phase has now moved on to the care-and-feeding-of-the-liver phase.

Until Monday then, take care.

Ken

P.S. I received a card from Gretchen the other day. On the front it shows a flock of very ordinary-looking sheep with one exception. One of the sheep has a very colorful bow tie on. The caption reads:

"Adding to my misery: No one here thinks I'm funny."

When you open the card, it reads:

"What is WRONG with these people?"

I thought, at least some of ewe might appreciate this!

CaringBridge Website
Monday, February 7, 2005

"Ken, your journal entry reminds me of the neutral zone in the 'Transitions' model by William Bridges. In his model, you start with an ending (leaving Rochester), go into a neutral zone, and end with a new beginning. The neutral zone is like the gap between the old and new—I always think of an acrobat letting go of the old trapeze and jumping off the platform to reach for the new one. The good news for you guys is that you have each other and a 'web' of family and friends to support you—your safety net!"

CaringBridge Guest Book
Fran and David, Minnesota

We are home. After three months, three weeks, and a day, we are home, and it feels good. Peg is very tired with all the traveling yesterday, and today we had a 7:30 AM blood draw in Tucson. This is the start of a new routine for us. The care and feeding of the liver at this point entails the following:

1. Weekly blood draws. These are done to check on liver functioning and the level of the antirejection drugs. Most of the tests can be analyzed locally. The antirejection drug blood sample is sent to Mayo. They monitor these and make any changes in Peg's medications as indicated.

2. Twice daily measurements of body temperature. These alert us to possible infection or rejection. We also have to check Peg's blood pressure because an elevated BP is a side effect of one of the drugs.

3. Daily medications. These change as needed as indicated

by the blood draws. Over time, the number of medications will be reduced, and hopefully, in about a year, Peg may have to take only one antirejection medication.

4. Diet restrictions are few. No alcohol, no caffeine, and no grapefruit juice are permitted.

5. Daily exercise. This is required to stay fit and tone up muscles that have atrophied over the past couple of years.

It is great to be home and be able to relax in our own surroundings. The past events have been so dramatic and so intensely emotional that we are, at this point, emotionally exhausted. We look forward to establishing some normalcy in our lives.

Ken

CaringBridge Website
Friday, February 11, 2005

If it hurts you
  to look back
 and frightens you
   to look ahead,
   then just look
    beside you...
     I'll be there

Hallmark Greeting Card

Another bump on this very bumpy road we are on. Tuesday morning Peg was running a high fever, and we had to go to an emergency room in Tucson. They sent her to the hospital, where she has remained. Tomorrow we fly back to Mayo in Rochester to be admitted to the hospital there. Right now she is okay to travel, so we want to get to Rochester ASAP.

The original concern was a blood clot in the leg. They eliminated that possibility, but the true diagnosis remains to be made. I imagine this will be a letdown for all of you, and as you might guess, we are so very weary of this road of complications.

I hope to get back into the Gift of Life Transplant House, but don't know yet.

I will keep you posted as soon as I can get to a computer. Please hang in there with us.

Ken

CaringBridge Website
Sunday, February 13, 2005

"My prayers continue for you both! May all the positive thoughts and prayers being sent your way act as arms holding you and helping to carry the added weight."

Caring Bridge Guest Book
Linda, Washington

Sorry to have taken so long to report in, but a lot has happened since we arrived here.

We got to Methodist Hospital at Mayo at 8:30 PM Saturday. They were ready for Peg, and by 9:45 PM, she had a meeting with a doctor, a blood draw, and a chest X-ray—all this on a Saturday night. What a place!

She was running a fever and had severe pain in her left leg. They have not arrived at a definitive diagnosis yet, but they believe it might be Valley Fever or coccidioidomycosis (what a mouthful that is).

Cocci, for short, is a disease that is regional to the Southwest. It is a fungus that lives in the soil, and most people who spend time there come in contact with it because the organism is airborne. Most folks don't get sick, or only mildly so, but some can get very sick. It can be deadly.

They theorize that Peg had the organism already in her body, and with the weakening of her immune system because of the antirejection drugs she is on, the cocci became an opportunistic disease. A final diagnosis will not be available for several days.

Tomorrow they will take a specimen from her lungs (she has several hundred spots on both lungs) and culture that. Additionally, they will do a bone scan. A blood test can be helpful in a final determination too.

There are some other possible causes they are considering (like tuberculosis), so they have her in a special room to prevent any spread of infectious organisms if she is contagious.

At this point, they are treating her as if she has Valley Fever, and it seems to be working. Her fever is down, and her leg hurts less. The leg pain may be from the possibility of the cocci fungus infecting her bones.

She is so very tired. She wasn't able to sleep because of the pain in her leg. Additionally, the antifungal drug has made her nauseous and has made her vomit fairly regularly. The poor gal. She has been through so much. She continues to fight. She is one tough lady.

I will keep you posted.

Ken

CaringBridge Website
Monday, February 14, 2005

Today Peg looks and feels a lot better. Her fever is gone, and the pain in her leg is greatly reduced. She had a CT scan this afternoon, and tomorrow she will have a three-stage bone scan, whatever that means. Then, either tomorrow or Wednesday, she will have a bronchoscopic procedure, where they will take some tissue samples from her lungs.

They have not made a final diagnosis, but the drug treatment she is on now seems to be working. It may be a while before they can make an accurate diagnosis because of the time required to grow cultures. She had nine visits from doctors today, two by individuals and the rest by teams.

I have just finished reading the book *The Doctors Mayo* by Helen Clapesattle, given to me by Kari, a friend and former student. The book is not only a history of the Mayo Clinic, but also a history of the development of medical treatment in this country. Fascinating reading. In it, the Father Mayo states that "no man is big enough to be independent of others." His philosophy is still obviously followed by today's staff. They are always collaborating and making team decisions. His words are not just words, but are observable behaviors we experience each day. As you might be able to guess, we are most impressed with this institution. There may be other places as good, but I would be willing to bet that there are none better.

Ken

P.S. If you end up at Mayo for treatment, be sure to mention my name. I get a piece of the action!

Peg and the Brothers Mayo

CaringBridge Website
Tuesday, February 15, 2005

Peg continues to improve. Today she had the three-stage bone scan. She was injected with a dye, and bone scans were taken over time—hence, the term "three stages." She started at 9:30 AM and was finished at 12:30 PM. She continues to get IV treatment with an antifungal drug, and this evening she received two units of blood. She will get the bronchoscopy late tomorrow afternoon. They continue to treat her as if she has Valley Fever, and as I said yesterday, it seems to be working.

It really is difficult for her to maintain her energy level given the schedule she is on. On one hand, they want her to eat, with special attention to protein intake, and to drink fluids. On the other hand, she can have nothing by mouth before her tests: no food or drink before the bone scan; no food or drink before the bronchoscopy. Go figure. She is still in the special environmentally controlled room until they can definitely rule out TB.

In addition to all this, the antifungal drug she is taking is wreaking havoc with the antirejection drugs. Apparently, the antifungal drug prescribed in Tucson was administered without reducing the dosage of the antirejection drug. The interaction between the two created the huge increase of the level of the antirejection drug in her blood stream. The doctor said he had never seen a blood level so high. The appropriate and desired level is between ten and twelve nanograms per milliliter. Peg's was in the high sixties. He also said that she would not have to worry about rejection—his idea of a joke, I guess. She is off the antirejection drug now until the level in her blood returns to a safe level. At this high level, it is extremely toxic, and they worry about kidney damage.

Our world is very small right now. Peg is tethered to an IV pole, and we take short walks in the hallways with a mask on. After they rule out TB, and I really don't think that that is a strong possibility, she can return to the transplant unit in Methodist Hospital. They will continue to closely watch her blood draws. No one has talked to us about the next step yet, so we just try to hang loose and focus on the next immediate challenge.

More tomorrow.

Ken

CaringBridge Website
Thursday, February 17, 2005

A better day. It looks like things are turning around. Peg has no fever, her leg is not hurting as much, and she was more alert and awake today. She will be returning to the transplant center tomorrow. TB has been ruled out, so we shed the masks.

We also learned some new information today. This may fall into the category of "more than I want to know about...," but Mayo did a pretransplant blood check for Valley Fever, and the test was negative. They do not know when Peg got the infection. However, they are guessing that the test result was a false negative or that the chemotherapy treatment she went through altered the test results. We will probably never know. They still do not know exactly what the infection is, but they know it is a fungus, and the drug they are treating her with is working.

It could take up to eight weeks to get a final definitive diagnosis. We now think that her nausea and vomiting was caused by the toxic level of the antirejection drug and not the infection. Each day the antirejection drug level in her blood drops but still remains unacceptably high. At least her stomach upset is gone. One doctor told us that we traded a terminal illness for a lifetime of medical management. An excellent trade.

Gretchen and Jo visited today. Gretchen looks great. She can now drive her car, and that makes a huge difference in her life. They brought homemade soup and hugs and kisses, all greatly appreciated.

Tomorrow.

Ken

CaringBridge Website
Friday, February 18, 2005

Peg has been moved to the transplant center in Methodist Hospital—Room 10-204. Some things have improved, and some have not. The level of the antirejection drug, Prograf, is now normal, and they start her on a low-level dose tomorrow. That is good. Her red blood cell count is back up to where it should be. That is good. Her kidney function is improving. That is good. Some of her blood chemistry is still out of whack (magnesium and potassium levels), and they are trying to correct that.

Today she ran a low-grade fever that was the result of the Valley Fever infection. It seems that treating this Valley Fever will be a long and slow process, probably lifelong. It is a difficult infection to eradicate, especially in someone with a compromised immune system.

Have you heard the saying, "Life is what happens while you are making other plans"?

Believe it!

Ken

CaringBridge Website
Saturday, February 19, 2005

A very long and slow day. Not much to report. Peg's fevers come and go. They rarely get over 100 degrees F and are usually not below ninety-nine. The doctors continue to monitor her closely, but she got a total break from medical tests and consultations today—no tests whatsoever, not even a blood draw.

She is getting up and moving more, although she is still getting IV fluids. I don't expect much to happen Sunday, but next week (maybe Monday), she will get an MRI on her leg, which continues to bother her. We both are very weary of all the bumps in the road. Please, no more bumps.

Today they started the Prograf medication at a very low dosage. It will be a case of trial and error to see what level she needs in concert with the antifungal medication. She will most probably be taking both medications for the rest of her life, one as a prevention for rejection and the other as a protection against the return of cocci.

I expect we will stay at the Gift of Life Transplant House after she is released from the hospital. We asked the doctors when that might be, but they couldn't say. It all depends on how well and how quickly she recovers from the infection.

The week of March 7 they will either remove the stents from her bile duct completely or replace them with larger stents. You can be certain that we will not return to Arizona before we are very comfortable with her health status. Who knows—if we stay here long enough the weather might even get nice! Take care.

Ken

CaringBridge Website
Saturday, February 26, 2005

Gretchen and Jo visited Friday. Gretchen looks absolutely terrific. She now looks as good as she did pretransplant—bright-eyed and bushy-tailed. Jo also looks as good as she did pretransplant—a no-nonsense, nose-to-the-grindstone, masochistic type of personal work-you-to-death trainer (just kidding). But seriously, Jo really is a very kind and loving person, a terrific caregiver, and a person with a wonderful sense of humor (just kidding).

We also had some friends from La Crosse visit today, which was great. Peg can stay with it for about two hours, and then she crashes. She can do about one thing each day. When we have something to do, we plan our day around that. That really makes having visitors very special.

Peg is looking better. Her blood chemistry is still not right and still requires extra attention. Mayo is very much attuned to the situation. Next week she has two tests scheduled, one of which is an MRI to check her leg. She will also see an orthopedic surgeon to see if there is anything else to be done besides the medication. The week of March 7, she will get a full battery of tests that are part of the protocol for posttransplant patients. If she had not gotten Valley Fever, we would have returned for these tests anyway.

It is hard to believe, but we are coming up on five months of being in Minnesota and Wisconsin, with the exception of the six-day interlude in Arizona. Back in October, we flew up here for what we thought was one week of testing. At that time, we learned about the possibility of receiving a "domino" liver transplant, which necessitated her staying close to Mayo.

A "domino" liver is a liver from an individual with a

chronic liver disease that is life threatening for that person but has taken many years to critically affect other organs. That liver needs to be replaced. However, it could function adequately in another person. Peg, at her age, would not be expected to develop the health problems caused by the donor's liver because the disease progression is so very slow. And so a suitable transplant liver for one person replaces the diseased liver that then goes to Peg—hence, the term "domino" liver.

We hope to go home sometime during March. We know from experience that we have to hang loose. We certainly do not want to return too early. Rochester is not exactly around the corner.

Everyone tells us that recovering from Valley Fever is a long, slow process, even for someone who isn't immunosuppressed. Peg needs to get plenty of rest each day. It will be a balancing act to get enough exercise to get in better physical shape and not have her muscles atrophy any further, and to get enough rest to recover from the Valley Fever. I guess we are talking about months, not days or weeks. She was doing really well posttransplant until this latest development.

It was tough to recover from this latest setback, but we are. All along the way during these past three-and-a-half years, we have had to continually adjust to bad news, so we know we can do it. You know what they say—"if it doesn't kill you, it makes you stronger." I keep wondering, however, if there isn't an easier way to get stronger. And what's so great about getting stronger anyway? How about just maintaining? And how about the status quo? Or how about not changing at all? Probably not!

I will return to the website next Saturday. By that time, we may have more to report. Other than that, it really is one day at a time.

Ken

P.S. Had a lot of snow here in Rochester. They clean it up really quickly. I know some people who actually like this stuff. Can you believe it?

....

CaringBridge Website
Saturday, March 5, 2005

Feels like the dog days of March. Each day, Peg improves. Each day, she seems to be ever-so-slightly better. To look back at yesterday, any change is almost imperceptible. To look back a week, the change is striking. There may be more unpredictable bumps in the road ahead (at this point, I have an emotional revulsion to the word "bump"). This constant concern of unpredictability might be what we can anticipate for our near future.

They tell us that four months out from the surgery, which for Peg will be April 22, a critical time period will have passed. After that, the one-year date is a landmark achievement. How these markers, or if these markers, are extended because of the complications Peg has experienced, we do not know at this time. I expect no one knows.

If you are getting tired of all this, rest assured that we most certainly are, too. Physically, we are exhausted. Emotionally and spiritually, we are exhausted. We, and I feel comfortable saying we, have been through so much that we are numb. It just feels like it would take too much energy to respond to anything at this point. On top of that is the haunting fear of the possibility of a new, unexpected negative event, another bump in the road. It feels as if we need to have something in reserve so we can respond if that were to happen. And so it goes.

Next week is a full week of testing. A major concern will be on Thursday when the bile duct stents will be removed, and the decision will be made to leave well enough alone or to insert two larger stents. Of course, if larger stents are inserted, that then would necessitate yet another return visit to have them removed.

People come and people go at the Gift of Life Transplant House. If you are here long enough, you can see how the community constantly changes. Most of the stories are good stories with happy endings. This regrettably is not always the case, and we lost some friends these past few days. It is emotionally wearing to be immersed in such drama all the time. As terrific as this place has been for us, we are both eager to leave.

More tomorrow.

Ken

....

CaringBridge Website
Sunday, March 6, 2005

A very good day. Yesterday we had four visitors from Eau Claire, and today Gretchen and Jo were here. In the morning, we heard Chaplain Mary Johnson give a presentation on "Disenfranchised Grief: Overlooking Losses That Shape Us." Very informative. We then went out to lunch and did some food shopping. Peg was out and about more today than she has been for a very long time. Our visitors all said that Peg looks a lot better than she did the last time they saw her. We are very anxious about next week with all the testing she will undergo. On top of all of this, the sun was shining, and the temperature was in the midfifties.

All in all, a very good day.

I would like to share with you some thought-provoking information from Mary Johnson's presentation. Disenfranchised grief is grief that a person experiences that is usually not recognized by others as a loss, for example, pet loss, death of a former spouse or partner, loss through retirement, physical losses, etc. Because of this, disenfranchised grief is more difficult to deal with and resolve.

Enfranchised and disenfranchised grief has a component called intrapsychic loss that involves the loss of the dream, the loss of "the way we thought it would be," and the loss of an emotionally important image of the self. It sounds a lot like what Peg and I are experiencing. Knowing it, claiming it, putting words and concepts to the experience enables us to gain more control over the situation. It permits us to think more clearly about the issue. It also seems to me that all of the losses involved in the very process of aging are included in the concept of disenfranchised grief. It was a very interesting presentation and provided much food for thought.

I will return on Wednesday when we will know more about Peg's situation.

Ken

CaringBridge Website
Friday, March 11, 2005

What a week! Thursday Peg woke up with the dry heaves. She was not able to eat anything on Wednesday because of the cholangiogram, and then took Darvocet for the pain, which most probably caused the upset stomach. Thursday she couldn't eat because of the ERCP, after which her nausea and dry heaves continued, probably due to the procedure itself and the general anesthetic. Today was another day of nausea and dry heaves, and another day of not eating. She spent the afternoon at the infusion clinic getting IV fluids so she wouldn't dehydrate. She has had a miserable week.

We met with the orthopedic surgeon this morning, and the recommended course of action is watchful waiting, and that is okay with us.

The ERCP was successful. They removed the 7 French- and 5 French-sized stents and replaced them with two 10 French-sized stents. A 10 French measures about three millimeters in circumference. They only go as high as a twelve. We have to return in twelve weeks to have these removed, at which time they will probably not insert any more stents. The stents have stopped the leakage from the bile duct and will allow the ducts to heal without closing up, hence the need for inserting larger stents.

Monday we see a lung specialist because they discovered another spot on her lung, yet another bump. We also meet with Dr. Poterucha. If all goes well, Peg may be released at that time. We know better than to count on anything at this point. I will return to the CaringBridge website on Monday after we have learned more. Hopefully, Peg will have a good weekend that will allow her to recover from all of this. Take care. —Ken

CaringBridge Website
Monday, March 14, 2005

The weekend provided Peg with a chance to recover, which she did. The nausea is gone and no more dry heaves. Thank goodness for that.

Initially, after the first diagnosis of Valley Fever, Peg's X-rayed lungs looked like a snowfall—many, many small white spots. Her lung X-rays have improved considerably. It is easy to see on the X-ray, even by us, that there are a lot fewer spots. Additionally, she has lost the persistent cough.

The new spot on her right lung, which is different than the other numerous spots on her lungs, is a mystery at this point, so they have scheduled another X-ray for tomorrow and another ultrasound, probably on Thursday. Neither are invasive tests, so that is good.

The pain in her legs continues, but it is less severe.

Dr. Poterucha continues to be "he who walks on water," as far as we are concerned. On Friday, when Peg was feeling so bad, he gave us his home phone and his cell phone and told us to call if she didn't get better. How many doctors do you know who would do that? Her blood work is not great, so Dr. Poterucha adjusted her medications. It really is trial and error as far as that goes.

We are learning to have no expectations now when we see the doctors. At this point, it is really the only way to handle the situation. Otherwise, you can waste a lot of nervous energy worrying, and that doesn't change a thing.

I was going to make a comment about this experience being a trip to hell and back, but I can't. We ain't back yet. I will return on Wednesday when we may know more.

Ken

CaringBridge Website
Wednesday, March 16, 2005

If you could see me now, you would see a great big smile on my face. Everything looks good. Peg is feeling better, and she got released from Mayo. It doesn't get any better than that. Almost all of her tests were good. The blood draw still shows some problems, but they can be addressed by adjusting the medications. This will be an ongoing and lifelong concern. It means that, for a while, Peg will have weekly blood draws. If all looks good, then this will become blood draws every two weeks, and then three, and so on. They will always be a part of our lifestyle, as will the two drugs Prograf and Fluconazole. We do not want to rush our return home.

We have a very good friend who also happens to be a librarian. Actually, this person happens to be my favorite (and only) sister-in-law. She butters me up by sending us books from time to time. I think she thinks it is a good way to keep me busy and out of trouble. So far so good. She recently sent me a most delightful read, *The No. 1 Ladies' Detective Agency* by Alexander McCall Smith. The main character is Mma Ramotswe, a wise and inventive woman. In discussing her relationship with doctors and some of her health concerns, she states that there is little that she would have problems with others knowing about except for constipation. I quote:

"Now constipation was quite a different matter. It would be dreadful for the whole world to know about troubles of that nature. She felt terribly sorry for people who suffered from constipation, and she knew that there were many who did. There were probably enough of them to form a political party—with a chance of government perhaps—but what would such a party do if it was in

power? Nothing, she imagined. It would try to pass leg-
islation, but would fail."

A good read and helps me to feel better about my
sharing with you *almost* everything!
Be back on Friday.

Ken

CaringBridge Website
Friday, March 18, 2005

> Anything we fully do is an alone journey.
> No matter how happy your friends may be for you,
> how much they support you, you can't expect anyone
> to match the intensity of your emotions
> or to completely understand what you went through.
>
> —Natalie Goldberg
> *Open Mind*, by Diane Mariechild

We are in a major snowstorm, the worst they have had in Eau Claire in recent memory. When it is expected to be over on Saturday, they are predicting from fifteen inches to twenty inches total accumulation. I actually forgot what fun it was shoveling snow—right.

It seems that Peg turned a corner this past Wednesday. Since then she has been eating better and moving better. It really looks like she is finally on a road to recovery. We feel very cautious at this point, but we are optimistically looking toward the future with our fingers crossed. We will delay our return to Arizona until Wednesday, March 23. We want to feel very comfortable with everything before we leave the security of being near Mayo.

What a journey this has been, not just the transplant but ever since the initial diagnosis in September 2001. I would say it has been an experience of a lifetime. I hope that Peg's recovery will be sure and steady. Only time will tell.

As I reflect on all that has happened, many thoughts come to mind. One is that with the passage of time, the intensity of what has happened will be diminished. It may become impossible to recapture the total, all-encompassing emotional rollercoaster ride we have been on. That is probably a good thing. I don't think I could continue to stay sane on a daily diet of all the highs and lows. With the passage of time, some sadness comes as the emotional drama of the past fades. It was an extremely intense and all-consuming moment that is being replaced with a satisfying calmness and a sense of perspective that can only come with distance and time.

I remember most vividly, after the apparent initial success of the transplant, an overwhelming feeling of joy and gratitude—joy for the possibility of more time with Peg and gratitude for everyone and everything that made this possible.

There are so many people, events, and experiences that have made this time in our life a miracle, and I have tried to share them with you as best I could. After living through these episodes, and with the passage of time, what was once considered a miracle and an almost unbelievable event can become acceptable and even sort of a commonplace event. I cannot let that happen. To do that would be to lose and to somehow diminish the truly wondrousness of this experience.

I cannot allow that to happen, and so I will always remember what a wondrous thing it is to be alive at a time when current medical techniques made a live liver donor an option for Peg. Had this occurred pre-2000, this would not have been the case.

What a wondrous thing to see Peg survive all the physical, emotional, and spiritual challenges placed upon her. How can I even come close to telling you what she has been through and what it must have taken for her to continue? No one can really understand what this has demanded of her, not even me. But I have seen her continually rise to the occasion and do whatever it takes to survive. What a wondrous thing.

What a wondrous thing to experience the love and support of our family of friends. This has been a surprise of unexpected responses. It has been truly revealing to see who has come forward and supported us in our time of need. There is an old Arabic proverb that speaks to the idea of a friend being one who can sift through the grain of friendship, separate the chaff from the seed, keep what is worth keeping, and with a breath of kindness, blow the rest away. When the chips were down, our friends came through and kept what was worth keeping, and with a breath of kindness, blew away the unimportant. This has been truly a marvelous thing to experience.

What a wondrous thing to contemplate a future with Peg. No one can know how much time we have left on this earth. Being alive, by definition, means that someday we must die. The hope is that the time given to us is lived fully and joyfully. That hope is what keeps us going. Hope is not the most important thing, but to paraphrase Vince Lombardi, the former Green Bay Packers coach, it is the only thing. Without hope, we lose the expectation of a tomorrow. Without hope, we can have no goals. Without hope, all is lost.

All of us who care about Peg have been given this hope for her and for us—a hope of a future, given to us through God, medicine, through Gretchen's gift, through Peg's tenacity for living, and through our life-sustaining and life-promoting relationships. What a wondrous thing!

I end with Hindu prayer *Namaste!* It sends the message to the heavens that says, "I celebrate the place in each of us where we are one."

Namaste!

Ken

CaringBridge Website
Sunday, April 3, 2005

"I read your thoughts about your reentry into normalcy after so long in combat-like circumstances. It sounded like postwar syndrome. Not only have you been dealing with your own life–death situation, but you have met many who are in similar situations. 'Normal' must seem a dream."

CaringBridge Guest Book
Jan and Jim, Wisconsin

We are home. I apologize for waiting so long to make this entry. It has been a combination of several things.

First, we were both physically and emotionally exhausted. The trip and the necessary activities to get our house up and running tired us both out. I would not be entirely honest to blame my laxity on only this, however. There were many times in the past five months when I was exhausted, and I still found the time and the energy to write.

The real problem is not that, but something quite different and more difficult to get a handle on. The problem is identifying and trying to understand who we are now and what we are now. The world has changed for Peg and for me. Much of the change has been unquestionably positive. Although this journey is far from over, it is no longer a journey of dread and insufferable waiting. We no longer have the same nagging questions. Will we find a donor? Will Peg be approved for the transplant? Will Gretchen be approved? When will it happen? Will it be successful? Will Gretchen be okay? Will Peg be okay? All of that has been answered, I am happy to say, in a very positive way.

Our questions and concerns are now quite different.

They deal with the medications, the watchful concern of Peg's recovery, the weekly blood draws that will for some time demand our attention, and the worry about the Valley Fever or any other opportunistic disease that decides to take up housekeeping in Peg's new body. The issue is one of, how do we live our life now? This is a strange land in which we find ourselves.

I have never been in the military service, and certainly have never experienced combat, but I wonder if what we are experiencing is not unlike the experience of those who have. We have been through a time in our lives for the past three-and-a-half years that has, for us at least, been unique. The past five months have been a daily dose of intense emotional survival. It was truly one day at a time. What new challenges will we face today? What new thing that we never heard of before will come and give us a whack on the side of the head? It always seemed to be a situation of get ready, be ready, stay ready!

The world has changed. Former activities that took our time and attention and were fun and interesting now seem different. How can I tell you this without putting anything down? It is not that these things have changed. It is that we have changed. We feel like we are in an emotional limbo. We feel numb. We feel disconnected. It feels like an emotional void.

I write about this not to gain your sympathy or even your understanding. I write about this to make a record of this time in our lives. You would think that after all we have been through that we would be joyful and ecstatic. Don't misunderstand. We are very grateful, and we feel very fortunate. Our life now will be different and unpredictable, and there are many unanswered questions still, but there is life! How wonderful to be able to say that. There is life!

I truly believe that this emotional limbo we are in

will change with time. Indeed, it is already changing. With the passage of time and with our engagement with friends and activities, things are looking up. Each day seems to be a balancing act with Peg's energy level and what we are able to do. As she continues to heal and gain back her strength, we will be able to do more.

They tell us it will take a year before she will start to feel like her old self again. She will actually never be her old self, but a new self with a new liver, ala Gretchen. Time will tell. I feel now, at least, time may be on our side.

At least, at last, we are home.

Ken

....

CaringBridge Website
Sunday, April 10, 2005

"Normal day, let me be aware of the treasure you are. Let me learn from you, love you, bless you before you depart. Let me not pass by in quest of some rare and perfect tomorrow. Let me hold you while I may, for it may not always be so. One day I shall dig my nails into the earth, or bury my face in the pillow, or stretch myself taut, or raise my hands to the sky and want, more than all the world, your return."

—Mary Jean Iron
A Grateful Heart, edited by M. J. Ryan

We have been home two weeks now. Things are settling down, and we are settling in. Mayo continues to advise us on how to adjust the medications. Peg has begun to physically work out once again, slowly and carefully beginning to build up her fitness level. You can imagine what a year of inactivity has done to her body. She has lost a lot of weight and has lost all of her muscle tone, but at least she has started on working to gain all that back. We have also started to pick up on our life here in Arizona. Our friends down here have welcomed us back with open arms, and it feels good.

Gretchen tells us she is wearing out the seat of her trousers from her butt dragging on the ground. She has just completed her first week of full-time teaching and finds it enjoyable but nonetheless tiring. For Gretchen and for Peg, it will be some time before their energy levels return.

We miss what we have left. Not the bad stuff. Not the uncertainty or the pain, both physical and emotional. We miss our friends up north who have been so supportive. We miss the closeness that comes with sharing such difficult times with people who care. We miss Gretchen, whose gift of life has made this present time possible. We miss Geri and John, who made us feel as if their home was our home too. We miss many more folks—and the list is long—who helped us through this difficult time. How very fortunate we are to have friends such as these.

Ken

P.S. The weather here reached a balmy 105 degrees F (but it is a dry heat) on our patio yesterday afternoon. I am glad to report that the ice has finally melted on the Santa Cruz River.

P.P.S. You know you are in Arizona when there are bridges and rivers…but no water!

The gals at "Fat Camp"

Cabin Mates and Ken. Front Row: Carole, Peg, Pam, Jo Ellen, Jane.
Back Row: Jo, Debbie, Rose, Justine, Toni, Geri,
Barb, Mary, Ken, Gretchen.

Friends "outstanding" in their field

Friends feed each other's spirits,
dreams and hopes; they feed each other
with the things a soul needs to live.

—Glen Harrington-Hall
stronger than cancer, by Connie Payton

What Are Friends For?

"Friends are like rainbows,
Heartsongs, and life...
They are a gift from God."

January 1997
"All About Friends,"
Celebrate Through Heartsongs,
by Mattie J. T. Stepanek

The phone rings:

   Peg: Hello?

   Caller: Peg, this is Gretchen. I have called Mayo, and I want to be your donor.

What are friends for? If we have learned nothing else on this transplant journey, we have learned the answer to this question.

Every year for the past fourteen years, Peg has attended a YMCA Fitness Camp for women in northern Wisconsin, called the Great Escape. It is an opportunity for women to spend time together in a beautiful setting where they can attend presentations geared to women, participate in arts and crafts, and of course, socialize, exercise, and eat healthy. That's the idea.

The women call it "Fat Camp." They spend most of their time socializing, exercising, and eating and eating and eating. Fat Camp.

Every year the makeup of the large group may change, but the group that Peg meets with remains essentially the same. This is the only time each year they are together as a group. All the women share some history, and some travel great distances to attend. One woman, Geri, has known Peg since they were ten years old. Another, Jo Ellen, gave everyone in the group a hope pendant, which Peg wears every day. Rose is the woman who gave me the Playboy calendar. The only year Peg missed camp was the year she had her first surgery.

Each year, the camp has a theme. The year after Peg's transplant, the theme was Survivor. What are friends for?

CaringBridge was a great way for me to get the information out about Peg. I could communicate everything at one time to everyone. What we didn't anticipate was that it also was a great way for our friends to communicate with us. During our four-month stay in Rochester, Minnesota, we received many hits on the CaringBridge website. Friends viewed the CaringBridge site more than eleven thousand times. They made more than two thousand entries in the Guest Book—entries of encouragement, entries of concern, entries to let us know they cared. What are friends for?

Peg received many cards from friends during this time— cards with sentimental poems, cards with funny pictures, cards that made her cry, cards that made her laugh. She keeps the cards in a wicker basket underneath the bed, underneath where she sleeps, so she can continue to receive the positive loving energy they hold for her. What are friends for?

Peg has a special place in our home where she goes to pray and meditate. It is her special place to quiet her mind and re-store her soul. In this special place, she has assembled special things given to her by friends. Ceramic angels, candles, dried flowers, a stuffed teddy bear, and poems are nestled together in this sacred place. What are friends for?

A friend had a prayer quilt with many tassels made for Peg, which was hung in her church. Whenever anyone said a prayer for Peg, they tied a knot in one of the tassels. We now have a quilt filled with knots on our living room sofa. What are friends for?

Peg's and Gretchen's surgery was not covered by our health insurance because the disease and transplant was considered experimental in her case. Friends helped us cover some of the medical expenses by contributing a tax deductable donation on their behalf to the National Transplant Assistance Fund. What are friends for?

We believe we have had approximately fifteen inquiries to Mayo about being a live donor for Peg. We don't know exactly how many because Mayo does not disclose this information. The process starts with a phone conversation with a transplant coordinator at Mayo. Age, blood type, and height of the person inquiring are the initial screening criteria. We only know if someone has called if they tell us they did. Only God and Mayo know how many actually did. What are friends for?

Friends are for loving.

CaringBridge Website
Monday, May 9, 2005

"...We'll be talking soon, and thank you again for teaching us to appreciate life more fully and to smell the flowers more often."

> CaringBridge Guest Book
> *Geri and John, Wisconsin*

Happy Mother's Day. We celebrated Mother's Day with Jane and Grandmother's Day with Peg.

I have just finished reading *I'm a Stranger Here Myself* by Bill Bryson. He makes me laugh out loud. In a chapter entitled "An Address," he tells of his speech to his son's graduating class, and he includes this "observation:"

"Take a moment from time to time to remember that you are alive. I know this sounds a trifle obvious, but it is amazing how little time we take to remark upon this singular and gratifying fact. By the most astounding stroke of luck, an infinitesimal portion of all the matter in the universe came together to create you, and for the tiniest moment in the great span of eternity, you have the incomparable privilege to exist. For endless eons, there was no you. Before you know it, you will cease to be again. And in between, you have this wonderful opportunity to see and feel and think and do. Whatever else you do with your life, nothing will remotely compare with the incredible accomplishment of having managed to get yourself born. Congratulations. Well done. You really are special."

To this I can only add—*Enjoy the ride!*

Ken

Such a Simple Thing

Verse 1

Such a simple thing
Like how your smile lights up a room
And our hands touch when we're alone
Your gentle smile when our eyes meet
It's then I know why I love you

Verse 2

Such a simple thing
Like when you watch a child at play
And how you brush your hair away
Your warm embrace when we kiss
It's then I know why I love you

Verse 3

Such a simple thing
Like when you wipe a tear away
And how you help a dog astray
Your open arms when friends you meet
It's then I know why I love you

Verse 4

Such a simple thing
Like how you move, the clothes you wear
And how your friends all know you care
Your phone calls when we are apart
It's then I know why I love you

Chorus

It's not the mountain but the stream
It's not the thunder but the gentle rain
It's how you wash my tears away
Then I know I love you.

—*Song lyrics by Ken Becker*

Such a Simple Thing

Ken Becker

Ken and Peg

She Loves Me, She Loves Me Not!

"Did you ever know that you're my hero?
And everything I'd like to be?
I could fly higher than an eagle
Cause you are the wind beneath my wings."

"Wind Beneath My Wings"
by Larry Henley and Jeff Silbar

Having a life-threatening illness changes everything, not the least of which is the level of intimacy you share with your partner. I am sure that what happens in a situation such as this is a direct result of the intimacy level the couple experienced before the life-changing event. It is impossible for me to generalize, but I can speak to our experience with some confidence and authority.

Peg and I have always had a close relationship, emotionally, spiritually, and physically. I can't tell you why or how this happened, but it seems to have always been present for us and, also, seems always to be changing. This closeness is the very heartbeat of our relationship. Peg's loving and caring for me and my loving and caring for Peg is the very core of us. That is what makes life worth living. At times, it feels like I don't know where I end and where Peg begins. When the threat of losing my partner was a distinct possibility, I found that our intimacy level was challenged.

At the emotional-spiritual level, our serious discussions about life and death and life after death have increased in number and intensity. We talked about these things before, but they were intellectual, philosophical discussions—dress rehearsals. Now these discussions were for real, as real as they get. We weren't talking about a future possibility but of a very oh-so-close reality. Nothing brings a clarity of thought and a drive to focus more dramatically than the imminent proximity of death. At these times, the unimportant and frivolous become known and identified for what they are. Precious time is no longer spent on unimportant things. Don't get me wrong. Not all discussions were heavy and laden with meaning, but when the time was right and we were ready, they were.

Intimacy at the physical level also changed quite suddenly and without warning immediately after the initial diagnosis and the first surgery. How can you have sexual feelings at times like these? These feelings, however, do not just go away, at least not for long. It has been said that to maintain a sexual relationship as one ages, a person needs an interesting and interested partner. For me, my wife has always been interesting and, until her diagnosis, interested.

As our love making became impossible for a variety of physical reasons, I found my response waning. My partner, always interesting, was no longer interested. Who could blame her? Aside from the physical pain and discomfort from her disease and treatment, any thoughts of joyful, pleasurable sexual times were often replaced with more somber and distressing thoughts about life and death, as you might imagine.

For me, this aspect of my life became a sad realization that what we had may be no more. Closeness now meant only holding and cuddling and crying together. As the saying goes, "Use it or lose it." I was afraid I was losing it.

We talked about this. We laughed and cried about this. We did the best we could without placing too many expectations on ourselves or each other. With the successful transplant, and with a slow but steadily improving energy level, our sexual health is also on a slow but steady path upward, if you pardon the expression. Thank goodness for that. We didn't lose it. We just set it aside for a while.

What She Brings

I hear the sound of her voice and my heart breathes
a sigh of relief
   I hold my breath as she speaks
      Her voice nourishes my soul, like the soft spring
      rain
      She lifts my soul
        My heart lightens with her every word
           She brings light to my dark,
              Calm to my storm
                  Peace to my soul in times of turmoil

She speaks to me not only with words, but also with
her eyes
   Her window to her soul
      I look into her soul with childish wonder
         She is beautiful inside and out
            She holds the child within me as the adult
            struggles to get out

Yet when I am with her, I am both child and man
   The best and worst of both worlds when we are
   together
      She is a link in the chain that binds me to this
      mortal earth
         Yes, we are bound together by forces we cannot
         explain
            Still trying to understand it
              We explore each other slowly,
                 Lovingly,
                    With much hope for the future

The Courage of One, by Joseph Kralicek

Some Days Are a Ten

Some days it seems that everything is absolutely perfect. Today is one of those days. The sun is shining. I am sitting by a northern Wisconsin lake, and a cool gentle breeze is blowing and caressing my face. I sit alone and enjoy the sensuous pleasure of being alive. I sit alone contemplating my life. I sit alone and know how very fortunate I am.

Not all days are a ten. Many have not even registered on the scale. You don't get to pick your number on any given day. The days just happen.

On the bad days, you just do the best you can. I have learned that on the good days I have to take notice. I let it in. I drink it in like a cool drink of water on a hot day. I savor the good days.

On a day like today, a ten day, I am a very lucky man. It might seem unlikely to say that, given our recent past, but things seem to be working out okay. After all is said and done, today is a ten day. I can see how much Peg's illness and her transplant have given me. You can imagine what they have given Peg and Gretchen.

Imagine how it feels to be Peg and to be alive because of a friend, when you were so close to death. Imagine each day as a precious gift to be lived fully, to be savored and consumed with gratitude, with awareness, and with a real sense of being alive, all because of a friend.

Imagine saving someone's life. A person you cared about was going to die without some intervention. Imagine having the courage to do that—to know unequivocally that Peg is alive today because of you. Imagine what Gretchen must feel.

Imagine having the person you love at your side. Imagine being me. I am a very lucky man.

Today is a ten. Come to think of it, now every day is a ten.

Postcript from Peg

As you can imagine this has been a most profound experience for me. I am a private person and I find it somewhat difficult to share such a significant event in my life in such a public way. To do so makes me feel very vulnerable. Beyond that there is the problem with words. Words cannot possibly describe the intensity and the variety of feelings I have experienced since 2001. Somehow to try to put words to the feelings attached to this journey is to not do this experience justice. Words, however, are all I have to work with and so, I begin.

My most constant companion is a feeling of being overwhelmed. I am overwhelmed with the love expressed, the compassion felt, and the mystery and miracle of it all.

I am overwhelmed with the true "Gift of Life" I have received from Gretchen. She says I have given her so much, but how do you thank someone for saving your life? I am humbled and cannot find the words to adequately express my heartfelt gratitude to her and what she has so graciously and courageously given me.

I am overwhelmed with my experience at Mayo. With my excellent surgeons Dr. Heimbach and Dr. Rosen, with Dr. Poterucha, with Chaplain Mary Johnson, and indeed the entire program. From start to finish they have been a very skilled and compassionate group of professionals. I always knew that this was where I wanted to be and I was right. I needed a miracle and through God, Grethcen, the Mayo Transplant Center, and the contintued support I receeived from family and friends, that a miracle and a second opportunity for life has been realized.

How do I find the words to share how much Ken means to me and how much he has sacrificed and done for me? Without him at my side I would not have survived. He is my inspiration. My sister, Jane, is a wonderful caregiver. She is always there when I need her; she never complains, she adjusts to my needs, and is a truly loving and giving person.

Humor has helped me through this journey. I have had some wonderful experiences with friends and laughter. Their humor and wit have brought me great joy. At times I laughed so hard that tears ran down my cheeks. I even have a dear friend who, dare I say, would on occasion "wet her pants" from laughing so hard. Thanks for the laughter.

I am overwhelmed by the love and kindness expressed by my family and friends. They have brightened my days and lightened my burden through cards sent, phone calls made, and visits and comments on CaringBridge. I can't find the words to express the powerful impact this has had on me. The fact that they have been part of my journey, the fact that they supported me and cared for me as they have is awesome! Each of them have been a very important part of my team. I don't know what I would have done without them. Thank You!

Please know how much I appreciate everyone's love and support. The hope they have continued to share with me has been incredible. With hope I have been able to meet the challenges of my cancer and the long involved process of the transplant experience. The "hope charm" that a special friend gave to me and some mutual friends to wear has been an important and significant tangible symbol of this hope. Thanks for giving me hope.

I believe in the power of prayer in the healing process. I can't help but believe that the prayers sent my way have had a positive influence on my healing process. Thank you for the prayers.

This has truly been a spiritual journey for me. I know my journey is not over and that I have only entered a new phase. Although I know that not everyone is as fortunate as I have been, I also realize that what happens to each of us is part of the mystery of life. I can only try to accept the gift of my new life with humility and with deep gratitude.

Words cannot come close to describing the depth of my appreciation but words are all I have...

Thanks SO very much,

Peg

Peg, spring 2005

Epilogue

"I do not have to believe in God, I know"

—C. G. Jung
Voices of Sedona, Lewis Tagliaferre

It has been almost three years since Peg's liver transplant. Her new liver continues to function perfectly, with occasional Mayo-directed changes to her daily medications.

Since November 2005, however, our journey continues to be neither easy nor smooth. There have been some very anxious moments as we have reacted and adjusted to these ongoing bumps in the road. The most recent development, however, has been very difficult. Her latest tests have shown that the carcinoid tumors have returned in her abdominal area. The looming question before us now is whether these tumors are fast growing or are slow growing. Only time will tell. The doctors told us after the transplant that they had "reset the clock." They estimated that Peg had had the carcinoid tumors for about ten years before they were detected. Resetting the clock meant that, optimistically, she had another ten years.

Peg continues to fight and to survive with dignity and grace. We continue to be engaged with our friends, our activities, and life, ever grateful for each new day we have together. If it were to come to pass that one of us dies before the other, I do not see that as an end to our relationship. It will only be a change in how we relate. I find that thought comforting. Until then, we continue to hope for the best...*one day at a time*.

Appendix A

Liver Transplant (LTx) Countdown

Three years, two months, and twelve days to transplant

September 18, 2001
LTx -1,167 days: First entered Gundersen Lutheran Hospital with severe abdominal pain. CT revealed lesions on Peg's liver.

September 21, 2001
LTx -1,164 days: Diagnosis of metastatic carcinoid cancer of the liver; primary site unknown.

September 25, 2001
LTx -1,160 days: First visit with Mayo gastroenterologist.

October 1, 2001
LTx -1,154 days: Surgery (exploratory) to locate primary carcinoid site; located and removed twelve inches from small intestine and some lymph nodes.

November 15, 2001
LTx -1,109 days: Met with oncologist; first approach to treatment — "watchful waiting."

April 3, 2002
LTx -970 days: Diagnosis changed from non-functional to functional carcinoid; discussion of next treatment; injections of octreotide.

November 2, 2002
LTx -757 days: Second approach to treatment; injections of octreotide.

February 27, 2003
LTx -663 days: Octreotide injections discontinued after four months of treatment; discussion of next treatment modality.

March 3, 2003
LTx -652 days: Third approach to treatment, chemotherapy.

July 29, 2003
LTx -512 days: Chemotherapy discontinued after four months of treatment; discussion of next treatment modality; admission sought to clinical trial of Iressa drug, taken orally.

February 5, 2004
LTx -321 days: Iressa medication initiated; admission to clinical trial finally approved.

March 31, 2004
LTx -266 days: Iressa medication discontinued; no other treatment modalities available; last visit with oncologist; first visit with transplant coordinating physician; decision to pursue transplant as last and only option.

June 2, 2004
LTx -203 days: First evaluation of transplant possibilities.

June 28, 2004
LTx -177 days: First donor evaluated and rejected.

October 18, 2004
LTx -65 days: Second evaluation for transplant.

November 11, 2004
LTx -41 days: Final approval for transplant; both donor and Peg given go-ahead.

December 3, 2004
LTx -19 days: Established surgery date, December 22, 2004; tentative based upon as-needed basis for surgery rooms.

December 22, 2004
LTx -zero: Transplant day.

TRANSPLANTED

References

Albom, Mitch. *tuesdays with Morrie*. New York, New York: Doubleday, 1997.

Betts, George. *Tears and Pebbles in my Pockets*. Millbrae, California: Celestial Arts, 1976.

Bryson, Bill. *I'm a Stranger Here Myself*. New York, New York: Broadway Books, 1990.

Burdman, Geri Marr. *Joyful Aging*. Mercer Island, Washington: Gerimar Publications, 1991.

www.Caringbridge.org; 3440 Federal Drive, Suite 100, Eagan, Minnesota, 55122; or (651)452-7940

Clapesattle, Helen, *The Doctors Mayo*, Rochester, Minnesota: Mayo Foundation for Medical Education and Research, 1990.

Gibran, Kahlil. *Patterns of Happiness*. Kansas City, Missouri: Hallmark Cards Inc, 1971.

Grana, Janice. *Images—Women in Transition*. Nashville, Tennessee: The Upper Room, 1976.

Henley, Larry and Silbar, Jeff. "Wind Beneath My Wings."

Kralicek, Joseph. *The Courage of One*. Chicago, Illinois: Grandoc Pub. Co., 2005.

Levy, Naomi. *Talking To God*. New York: Doubleday, 2002.

Maier, Frank. *Sweet Reprieve*. New York, New York: Crown Publishers Inc., 1991.

Mariechild, Diane. *Open Mind*. San Francisco, California: Harper, 1995.

My Journal. Rochester, Minnesota: Mayo Clinic, Mayo Foundation For Medical Education and Research, 1998.

National Transplant Assistance Fund, 150 N. Radnor Chester Road, Suite F-120, Radnor, PA 19087. 1-800-642-8399.

Oregon Quarterly. Eugene, Oregon: Autumn 2005; taken from *A Certain World*, by W. H. Auden

Payton, Connie, *stronger than cancer*. Lynnwood, Washington: Compendium Inc., 2002.

Prather, Hugh. *I Touch The Earth, the Earth Touches Me*. Garden City, New York: Doubleday and Co. Inc., 1972.

———. *Notes to Myself*. Moab, Utah: Real People Press, 1970.

Prather, Hugh, and Gayle Prather. *Notes to Each Other*. New York, New York: Bantam Book, 1990.

Proverbs for Daily Living. Mount Vernon, New York: The Peter Pauper Press.

Remen, Rachel Naomi, M.D. *Kitchen Table Wisdom*. New York, New York: Riverhead Books,1996

Roberts, Elizabeth, and Elias Amidon. *Prayers for a Thousand Years*. New York, New York: Harper San Francisco, 1999.

Roosevelt, Eleanor. *Bartlett's Familiar Quotation*. Boston, Massachusetts: Little Brown Company, 1980.

Ryan, M. J. *A Grateful Heart*. York Beach, Maine: Conari Press, 1994.

Smith, Alexander McCall. *The No. 1 Ladies' Detective Agency*. New York, New York: First Anchor Books, 2002.

Stepanek, Mattie J. T. *Celebrate Through Heartsongs*. New York, New York: Hyperion, 2002.

Smyth, Mary Cathrine. *A Wee Thought*. Mt. Jackson, Virginia.

Tagliaferre, Lewis. *Voices of Sedona*. Springfield, Virginia: C-E-C Group, 1996.

Zdenek, Marilee. *Splinters in my Pride*. Waco, Texas: Word Books, 1979.

Ken Becker, author

About the Author

Dr. Kenneth C. Becker, DEd, is a professor emeritus who was chair of the Department of Health Promotion and Health Education and taught at the University of Wisconsin— La Crosse for more than twenty-seven years. His expertise is in the area of mental health, counseling, human sexuality, communication skills, and philosophy. He is a Gestalt therapist and owned a counseling agency with his wife, Peg Dosch. Both he and his wife are retired and living in Arizona. He has been his wife's primary caregiver since she was first diagnosed with cancer in 2001.

Printed in the United States
88501LV00003B/271-309/A

9